CLAIMING OUR INHERITANCE

The boundary lines have fallen for me in pleasant places;
surely I have a delightful inheritance.
Psalm 16:6

To Les ~
with much gratitude
for your ministry to Jim
and all of us at his
service ~ God bless you and
your continuing ministry,
Candy
†

CLAIMING
OUR
INHERITANCE

A STUDY IN COLOSSIANS

CANDACE BROWN DOUD

Xulon Press

Xulon Press
2301 Lucien Way #415
Maitland, FL 32751
407.339.4217
www.xulonpress.com

Scripture quotations taken from the Holy Bible, New International Version (NIV). Copyright
© 1973, 1978, 1984 by International Bible Society. Used by permission of Zondervan. All
rights reserved.

All hymns quoted are in the public domain.

Printed in the United States of America.

ISBN-13: 9781545635933

To my grandchildren:
Brooke, Tate, Daniel, Jacqueline, Isabella, Parker, John, Matthew,
Hunter, and Grace and great-grandchildren: Luke and Jonathan.
You have a priceless inheritance.

Table of Contents

Dear Reader,

Are you tired of trying to keep up with the hectic, increasingly impossible demands of the twenty-first century? Are the hi-tech gadgets we have created overtaking and controlling your life? Are the events of our time depressing you? Are you deprived of time, space, energy, sleep, and peace? Do you long for freedom from the stress and anxiety of this self-imposed lifestyle?

It's time to take a break, step back, and reflect on what God has provided for us so we can recharge our batteries, reset our focus, and center our thinking on Him because time is running out. Jesus is coming back and we want to be ready when He comes, but we also want to take full advantage of all He offers us in the meantime.

Claiming Our Inheritance is a summary of the resources Jesus has left to all people of every generation. But every individual must come forward and claim them for himself. Based on the Book of Colossians, but drawing on other Scriptures as well, we will explore our inheritance, learn how to claim it, and be motivated and equipped to live wisely because of it.

This book is dedicated to you, the reader, while we eagerly wait for Jesus to return.

Candace Brown Doud
Sequel to *Waiting His Return* published in June 2015 by Xulon Press

Introduction

*A*t the time of death, a person's Will is considered legal and binding provided the document has been prepared correctly and executed according to the jurisdiction of the deceased. At that time, the beneficiaries are notified and given a certain time frame to come forward and claim their inheritance.

Upon Jesus' death, all the prophecies concerning Him in the Old Testament, and every word He spoke and every promise He made in the New Testament, became His Last Will and Testament to people of all generations who put their faith in Him. It is a rich inheritance. It is an inheritance that not only determines our eternal destiny but also determines how we live in the present.

In his letter to the church in Colossae toward the end of the first century, the Apostle Paul summarizes this inheritance for us. His assessment lends itself to being a perfect handbook for Jesus' beneficiaries not only in Paul's day but for people in every age, including those of us living in the twenty-first century. Paul helps us catch our breath and pay attention to the things that really matter. Therefore, this book is written with the hope that it will be referred to often to strengthen and encourage, to inspire and motivate, to convict and challenge, to grow personally, and to share with others because, unlike any other inheritance we may receive in our lifetime, this inheritance is available to all who claim it and its resources never end. They stretch forth into eternity.

Chapter 1

The Gift of Salvation

*W*e can't possibly appreciate the gift of salvation or comprehend the value of the inheritance it offers without going
back to the very beginning.

Our story begins there in a garden, an indescribably beautiful
garden, alone with God. Our parents, Adam and Eve, were the
epitome of God's creation, created in His image to have fellowship
with Him and bring Him glory. The garden was a perfect environment: ideal climate, luscious fruit, streams of fresh running water,
animals for fun and companionship and, most of all, the presence
of God Himself.

Unfortunately, Satan, the archenemy of God, interrupted this
perfect picture and changed man's relationship with God forever.
Adam and Eve had chosen to listen to and obey Satan rather than
listen to and obey God. Known as the Fall of Man, this episode
introduced sin and death into the human race. We can describe
sin as any behavior in thought, word, or deed that violates God's
perfect standard or misses the mark He set for us. Adam and Eve
missed the mark that day. Sin became the great divide between
a holy God and now, a genetically sinful humanity. The consequences of their disobedience were huge. Banned from the garden
and the presence of God, Adam and Eve and every future generation had to work the land for food and shelter. Pain, suffering, wars,

and conflict became part of life. Death became a merciful ending to life that should have been eternal.

Fortunately, our story does not end there. The amazing truth is God knew this outcome even before it took place. He had a plan to restore our relationship with Him because His desire all along was our companionship. That plan unfolds for us in the Bible. It is the story of His intense love for His creation and the story of His zeal to win us back to Him so we can spend eternity with Him. The central figure is His Son, Jesus Christ. The central theme is the cross on which He died. God sent Him as the only acceptable way to deal with the sin problem we all experience. God sent Himself in human form to become the atoning sacrifice for the sins of the world. That is why the cross stands in the center of human history and beckons us to it.

God has provided the way, the only way, back into relationship with Him. Without the cross, we are defaulting to Satan. The cross bridges the gap, pays the debt our sin incurs, and sets us free. This is the gospel. This is the good news we have in Jesus Christ. This is the gift of salvation He offers each one of us.

Here is our inheritance: Salvation from sin (any act of disobedience against God) is available to everyone through the shed blood of Jesus Christ.

Paul experienced this incredible reality for himself on the Road to Damascus. He was an enemy of Christ. He was a staunch Jew, a Pharisee determined to wipe this new sect of believers off the map. But all that changed in a flash of lightning when Jesus appeared to him and rechanneled his energy and commitment in the right direction. Thus, Saul of Tarsus became the great Apostle Paul, writer of this letter to the church in Colossae and twelve other books in the New Testament. His writings reveal one of the greatest minds that ever lived, and he spent the rest of his life teaching, preaching, writing, and living out his faith so that others might believe as well.

We meet Paul here, near the end of his life, imprisoned in Rome for sharing the gospel. But nothing will stop him from following through with that commitment. So when he hears that some false teachers have infiltrated the church in Colossae and are telling believers they should be open to other teachings because faith in Jesus isn't enough, Paul wastes no time writing this letter to set the record straight. Faith in Jesus IS enough, and our inheritance of salvation is proof. Paul outlines this truth for them and for us so we will not be dissuaded from this basic tenet of our Christian faith.

We have the privilege of reading this letter two thousand years later. If you've never met Paul through his other writings, these believers in Colossae hadn't either so he begins by introducing himself before presenting this gift, the gift of salvation, the first installment of our inheritance.

The Bible says Paul wrote:

> Paul, an apostle of Christ Jesus by the will of God, and Timothy our brother, to the holy and faithful brothers in Christ at Colossae: grace and peace to you from God our Father. We always thank God, the Father of our Lord Jesus Christ, when we pray for you, because we have heard of your faith in Christ Jesus and of the love you have for all the saints–the faith and love that spring from the hope that is stored up for you in heaven and that you have already heard about in the word of truth, the gospel that has come to you. All over the world this gospel is bearing fruit and growing just as it has been doing among you since the day you heard it and understood God's grace in all its truth. You learned it from Epaphras, our dear fellow servant, who is a faithful minister of Christ in our behalf, and who also told us of your love in the Spirit. (Colossians 1:1-8)

Knowing Our Inheritance

The death, resurrection, and ascension of Jesus Christ several decades earlier was the "Breaking News" of the day. Even without modern technology and social media, it was spreading like wildfire because people were desperate. They were desperate for hope, desperate for the truth, and desperate for a future. This monumental event divided history and changed the world forever. What happened in the city of Jerusalem on that fateful weekend was quickly becoming known all over the world as lives were changed for all eternity. The Roman government in control at the time couldn't stop it. The Jewish religious leaders who refused to accept Jesus as their long-promised Messiah or deliverer from Roman occupation couldn't stop it. The masses of people from all backgrounds and nationalities who protested against Jesus couldn't stop it. This news was unstoppable! Jesus knew it would be, so He had commissioned His eleven faithful disciples to go and make disciples of all nations, baptizing them in the name of the Father and the Son and the Holy Spirit, and teaching them to obey everything He had commanded them (Matthew 28:19-20). After appointing Matthias to take the place of Judas Iscariot who betrayed Jesus, the twelve had done just that.

Now even though Paul, who called himself the "abnormally born" apostle because he was not one of the twelve (1 Corinthians 15:8), is sidelined from continuing his own efforts to preach the gospel, God never wastes the love and commitment of His servants. He had chosen Paul for this purpose, and His purposes will always prevail. Paul's life proves that to be true. Who would have ever guessed this single letter written in approximately 60 AD would bless so many people for so many centuries? Paul certainly didn't, and this little group of believers in Colossae certainly didn't. Yet as it turns out, they represent believers in every age. It is crucial we understand what Paul is telling them and, in turn, us.

Saints are people of all generations who have accepted the free gift of salvation that Jesus Christ offers us on the cross. Therefore, saving faith, or the only kind of faith that has the power to save us, is faith in Him and in the sacrifice He made on our behalf. This is our great hope in a world dominated by Satan and the evil he perpetuates to destroy and distract us from God.

Heaven is our eternal home with God and the final destination of all believers.

The word of truth is the Bible, God's written Word to mankind. Though written over a period of fifteen hundred years by forty different writers, it was inspired by God Himself (2 Timothy 3:16). It is the story of our redemption from beginning to end, from Genesis to Revelation.

4

The gospel is the good news of our salvation in Christ. It is only available to us by God's *grace*, or His favor toward us that we could never earn or acquire on our own and certainly don't deserve. This is the *truth* the world was desperate to hear in Paul's day, and it is the truth people are desperate to hear today.

Receiving Our Inheritance

The gift of salvation is based on our need as sinful people and God's abundant provision in sending His Son to die so that we can live. But just like we have to open the legal document informing us of an earthly inheritance, we must open this gift Jesus offers us. Simply knowing He existed and He died and rose again is not enough to save us from our sins. We must transfer that head knowledge into a heart transformation that leads to a personal transaction. We acknowledge our sinfulness before Him and our inability to save ourselves and then recognize and accept His sacrifice on our behalf. At that moment in time, we become justified in God's court of law. In other words, we are declared, "Not Guilty!" Our sins are forgiven. God looks at us and instead of seeing our sins and having to judge us accordingly, He sees the blood of His Son. And the debt we owe for our sin is marked, "Paid in Full!"

The Apostle John gives us the foundation for this transaction:

> For God so loved the world that He sent His one and only Son that whosoever believes in Him will not perish but have everlasting life. (John 3:16)

Paul maps out this truth for us in his letter to the Romans:

> No one is righteous, not even one. (Romans 3:10)

> All have sinned and fall short of the glory of God and are justified freely by his grace through the redemption that came by Christ Jesus. God presented him as a sacrifice of atonement through faith in his blood. (Romans 3:23-25)

5

The wages of sin is death but the gift of God is eternal life for those who are in Christ Jesus. (Romans 6:23)

Salvation from sin is the first rung of the ladder in reconciling sinful people to a holy God. God set the plan in motion and, at the appointed time, came Himself in human form to execute that plan in the Person of Jesus Christ. The cross becomes the crossroads for every human being to meet God on His terms. We must accept the sacrifice He made on our behalf. There is no other way to be saved. There is no other way to deal with the sin problem that infects all of humanity. Any attempt to come to Him another way is impossible because God created us to be with Him, and God sent His Son to redeem us from sin so we could. There will always be false teachers preaching a false gospel to people who want to hear the fake news that they can find their own way to God. But that is the epitome of Satan's deceit and human pride.

Jesus makes it very clear who He is and why we need Him:

I am the bread of life.

I am the light of the world.

I am the gate.

I am the good shepherd.

I am the resurrection and the life.

I am the way and the truth and the life.

I am the true vine. (from John 6-15)

God initiates our relationship with Him, but we must surrender to His supremacy and authority by understanding and accepting Jesus for who He is—God in the flesh, born to set us free from the bondage of sin. That is why our personal transaction with Him is called being born again. We are born physically at birth, but we are spiritually dead until we come to Jesus. In John 3:7 Jesus says, "You must be born again." So without spiritual birth, we remain dead in our sins (Ephesians 2:1). But receiving the gift of salvation brings us to life now and for all eternity.

If you have not made this transaction and received God's gift of salvation, now is the time. God has led you to this book and wants you to come to Him. He has so much in store for you. Find a quiet place and bow your head and your heart before Him, and say this simple prayer or something similar:

> Dear Jesus, thank you for guiding me to this life-changing truth. I recognize I am a sinner before you, and I cannot save myself from sin. I need and gratefully accept your sacrifice on the cross on my behalf. I know now you paid the debt for my sin, and therefore I am no longer condemned by it. You took my condemnation for me. Thank you, Lord Jesus. Help me live in that reality from this day forward. Amen

Now you are a child of God and, as such, entitled to your full inheritance. Welcome to the family!

Bible verses to consider on salvation:

> Salvation comes from the Lord. (Jonah 2:9)

> The Lord is my light and my salvation. (Psalm 27:1)

> His salvation is near those who fear Him. (Psalm 85:9)

> Turn to me and be saved. (Isaiah 45:22)

> There is no other name under heaven given to men by which we must be saved. (Acts 4:12)

> He alone is my rock and my salvation. (Psalm 62:2)

> By the gospel you are saved. (1 Corinthians 15:2)

God, who is rich in mercy, made us alive with Christ even when we were dead in transgressions—it is by grace you have been saved. (Ephesians 2:4-5)

God wants all men to be saved and to come to a knowledge of the truth. (1 Timothy 2:4)

My salvation will last forever. (Isaiah 51:6)

How shall we escape if we ignore such a great salvation? (Hebrews 2:3)

Let us rejoice and be glad in His salvation. (Isaiah 25:9)

And the Apostle Peter adds:

Like newborn babies, crave pure spiritual milk, so that by it you may grow up in your salvation, now that you have tasted that the Lord is good (1 Peter 2:2).

Our salvation from sin in Christ leads us in a brand new direction. It is the beginning of a brand new life, and it is important we work it out in the way we live.

Living Our Inheritance

God does not save us from sin and just turn us loose to figure out the benefits for ourselves. We will spend the rest of this book learning how these benefits affect our lives, but suffice it to say here, we have a whole new outlook on life. We are no longer alone trying to navigate in our own strength.

We have new energy, new purpose, new focus, new desires, and new hope.

We are more aware of our environment, the world we live in, the role we play, and other people and things that really matter.

We are more caring, compassionate, understanding, and forgiving.

We are sensitive and protective of our spiritual blessings.

We desire the things of God because God Himself is living in us, and we have all His resources at our disposal. That separates us and acts as a shield from the unbelieving world around us. Receiving the gift of salvation defines our life from that point forward and becomes an irrevocable inheritance.

Personal Reflection

I grew up in an alcoholic home and the only time I heard God's name was when it was used to swear. And yet, there were many opportunities to know God and I grabbed every one of them because I knew deep down He was there, and I longed to know Him. I was fortunate to go to a Catholic high school that encouraged that pursuit in that I learned to have a healthy fear or reverence for Him I never would have had otherwise. But it took a life-threatening illness to help me understand He didn't just want me to know about Him, He wanted me to know Him.

That conviction led me to Bible Study Fellowship where I learned you can't possibly know God without studying His Word to us, the Bible, and learning Jesus is God in the flesh, sent to this earth for people just like me who were searching for Him. I was thirty years old, and sitting in that Bible study class, when I opened my heart to receive this most precious gift. My decision that day was the turning point in my life. Everything I have said so far in this book and everything I say in the rest of it is written from my perspective now, after forty-five years of following Jesus. God does not lie, and everything He promises in His Word is ours as His children. There is simply no better way to live and to die than knowing beyond a shadow of a doubt He loves you with an everlasting love, you are forgiven for your sins, and you are saved by the blood of Jesus Christ for all eternity.

Personal Thoughts and Study Guide

1. Have you received the gift of salvation Jesus died to give you?

2. Describe your moment of decision and the value of this inheritance to you personally.

3. How would you introduce yourself to an audience you have never met?

4. Re-write Colossians 1:3-6 from your own perspective to thank God for the people who have encouraged you in your faith.

5. Define these phrases from your own experience:

Faith in Christ

Hope stored up for you in Heaven

Word of truth

Bearing fruit

God's grace

Make It Your Own

Which Bible verse on salvation will you memorize as your go-to verse to help someone else receive God's gift of salvation? Write it down to help you remember it.

Hymns of the faith contain great doctrinal truths and bring us much comfort and peace.

This one speaks of God's love and our salvation:

And Can It Be
by Charles Wesley

> And can it be that I should gain
> An int'rest in the Savior's blood?
> Died He for me who caused His pain?
> For me, who Him to death pursued?
> Amazing love! How can it be,
> That Thou my God, shouldst die for me?

Chapter 2

Access to the Throne

𝒯he gift of salvation changes our relationship with God forever. We now have direct access to Him through the shed
blood of Jesus Christ. We stand in His grace redeemed and forgiven.
Therefore, we have direct and personal communication with Him.
This is prayer. It is our great privilege as believers.

Here is our inheritance: Prayer is our lifeline to God.

Paul has taken full advantage of this relationship since the
day he first met Jesus on the Road to Damascus decades earlier.
He takes full advantage of it now when he hears false teaching is
threatening the church in Colossae. He assures the believers of his
continued prayer for them to avoid these errors and to stay focused
on the truth they have been taught.

The Bible says Paul wrote:

> For this reason (their faith), since the day we heard about
> you, we have not stopped praying for you and asking God to
> fill you with the knowledge of his will through all spiritual
> wisdom and understanding. And we pray this in order that
> you may live a life worthy of the Lord and may please him

in every way: bearing fruit in every good work, growing in the knowledge of God, being strengthened with all power according to his glorious might so that you may have great endurance and patience, and joyfully giving thanks to the Father, who has qualified you to share in the inheritance of the saints in the kingdom of light. For he has rescued us from the dominion of darkness and brought us into the kingdom of the Son he loves, in whom we have redemption, the forgiveness of sins. (Colossians 1:9-14)

Knowing Our Inheritance

Paul knows firsthand what it is like to be rescued "from the dominion of darkness" and forgiven by Jesus Christ. This is the very crux of the gospel. His prayer shows his total transformation from being a legalistic Jewish Pharisee, the strictest arm of the Jewish ruling council in Jerusalem, who at one point wanted to kill these new Christian converts, to now leading them and being determined to protect the truth of the gospel. Paul loves Jesus, he loves His gospel, and he loves His church. This love can only come from God. This love is fiercely committed to Him and to His kingdom. And this love is always proven by our willingness to pray.

Paul prays for these believers:

> To have God's wisdom and understanding.
> To live a life worthy and pleasing to the Lord.
> To bear fruit in every good work.
> To grow in their knowledge of God.
> To be strengthened in Him.
> For endurance and patience.
> For joyful gratitude.
> To know their inheritance as part of the Kingdom.
> To always remember how they were rescued from the darkness by Jesus who has redeemed them and forgiven them.

These are the essential ingredients to living the Christian life and they mark the distinction between believers and unbelievers. Paul frames this prayer between two bookends. The first bookend is spiritual wisdom and understanding because God's wisdom is different than ours, and we cannot have it without first receiving His gift of salvation. Paul knows these believers have accepted this gift, so from that basic foundation, he now prays for them to move forward in their faith; to be good ambassadors for Jesus Christ and to live a life worthy of His calling; to not rest on their salvation but to be productive for His Kingdom; to not be content with where they are spiritually but to grow and mature in their faith; to continually draw their strength from Him because it produces endurance and patience; and to be joyful and thankful in all situations because our joy and gratitude are rooted in Him and not in our circumstances.

These ingredients of our faith come from knowing we belong to God through Jesus Christ and, therefore, we are entitled to our inheritance. Knowing whose we are helps us become who He created us to be. Paul wants these believers in Colossae and all believers since to be resolutely aware of the endless possibilities we possess because of the open access to God we now have through Jesus Christ. So it only stands to reason the other bookend at the end of Paul's prayer is this reminder: remember what Jesus did for you and celebrate it every day. Never forget how He rescued you from the kingdom of darkness or the kingdom of this world. He purchased you from that world of sin with His precious blood and placed you in His Kingdom. Your sins are not only forgiven, they are forgotten (Psalm 103:12). He invites you to come into His presence and He delights in answering your prayers.

Paul's prayer is for our benefit as well. These essential ingredients to our faith are available to us upon request.

The Bible says:

> We can ask God for wisdom and He will give it to us. (James 1:5)

> We can live a life worthy of His calling. (Ephesians 4:1)

> We can be productive in His Kingdom. (Matthew 7:16)

> We can mature in our faith. (2 Peter 3:18)

We can draw strength from His Word. (Psalm 119:28)

We can develop endurance and patience in our sufferings. (2 Corinthians 1:6)

We can let our joy overflow and be thankful in all situations. (Habakkuk 3:18; 1 Thessalonians 5:18)

We can understand, accept, and live out our inheritance in His Kingdom. (Deuteronomy 4:20; Hebrews 9:15)

We can serve God while we wait for Him to return to judge the world. (1 Thessalonians 1:10)

And we can look back and always remember what Jesus did for us.

In Him and in Him alone, we have redemption and forgiveness for our sins. (Ephesians 1:7)

It also helps us look back to the Old Testament and understand man has always prayed to God and God has always heard the prayers of His people. The first recorded prayer in the Bible occurred after Adam and Eve's son Cain killed his brother Abel. The response to the evil this generated was, "men called on the Lord" (Genesis 4:26). Moving forward throughout the Old Testament, giants of the faith like Abraham, Moses, Joshua, Naomi and Ruth, Samuel and David, Solomon, Esther, Job, and Daniel (just to mention some of the obvious) prayed, and God heard their prayers. But in the Old Testament, man's relationship with God was external.

In the New Testament, Jesus brought prayer to a whole new level. We can now know the God we pray to. He becomes personal to each believer. We can approach God's throne with confidence because Jesus has removed the barrier of sin that existed between us. He has bridged the gap and reconciled us to Him. He even gave us a visual aid to prove it. At the exact time of His death, the huge curtain inside the Temple in Jerusalem split in two from top to bottom (Matthew 27:51). This was a sign to the world going forward that a new relationship between God and man had begun.

We now have direct access to God because of what Jesus did for us on the cross. The door to His throne room is always open. His line is never busy. We are never put on hold and told how many people are in line ahead of us. He is available anytime, anywhere and can handle all of our prayers at once.

So our response to the evil we face today is the same — we turn to the Lord and pray. We have seen it in our own lives on our TV screens after terrorist attacks, mass shootings, natural disasters, and world pestilences and famine have threatened our world. Prayer is our go-to response. It is the natural thing to do. God created us in His image with a vacuum only He can fill. At the deepest level we know that to be true regardless of our spiritual background, so when confronted with evil, uncertainty, and fear with no place else to go, we turn back to God.

Thoughts on Prayer:

Prayer is the great privilege of every believer as a child of God.

Prayer puts all God's resources at our disposal.

Prayer makes us a part of God's work here on earth.

Prayer connects us to other believers.

Prayer puts our life and circumstances in proper perspective.

Prayer changes us before it changes who or what we are praying for.

Prayer takes the responsibility off us and puts it on God.

Prayer is the great stress reliever.

Prayer rejuvenates us and gives us hope.

Prayer brings comfort and peace.

Prayer equips us for what God calls us to do.

Prayer makes us homesick for Heaven.

Receiving Our Inheritance

Before Jesus left this earth, He told His disciples it was for their good He was leaving them because He would send the Holy Spirit to live in them as their direct line of communication with Him (John 16:7-15). This promise was fulfilled seven weeks after Jesus' resurrection on the Day of Pentecost. Hundreds of people were gathered and experienced this historical and life-changing event (Acts 2). Today, two thousand years later, countless millions have had the same experience. When we receive Jesus Christ as our Lord and Savior, the Holy Spirit of God moves in and takes up residence in us, giving us this direct access to God Himself. It is a beautiful picture of the Triune Godhead—Father, Son, and Holy Spirit—working together on our behalf.

This is what separates Christianity from every other religion in the world. We love, worship, follow, serve, and pray to this God, the living God. This is how much He desired us to know Him. This is how much He wanted to be part of our lives. This is how much He wanted 24/7 contact with us. That's why prayer is such a privileged inheritance, and that's why once we claim it, our lives are never the same again.

Bible verses to consider on prayer:

God hears our prayers from His holy heaven. (2 Chronicles 30:27)

God hears my cry for mercy and accepts my prayer. (Psalm 6:9)

O you who hear prayer, to you all men will come. (Psalm 65:2)

Prayers of the upright please him. (Proverbs 15:8)

Before they call I will answer; while they are still speaking I will hear. (Isaiah 65:24)

Whatever you ask for in prayer, believe you have received it and it will be yours. (Mark 11:24)

The eyes of the Lord are on the righteous and his ears are attentive to their prayer. (1 Peter 3:12)

If my people who are called by my name will humble themselves and pray and seek my face and turn from their wicked ways, then will I hear from heaven and will forgive their sin and will heal their land. (2 Chronicles 7:14)

What awesome promises. And Jesus invites us to share this inheritance.

Living Our Inheritance

For the believer, praying to our God who has demonstrated His love to us in such powerful and life-changing ways, should be as natural as breathing. How can we begin our day, end our day, or face any situation in between without looking to Him first in gratitude that He is there and that He cares, and then for the help we need to move forward? Only Jesus walked this earth as one of us. Only Jesus knows our deepest needs. He experienced more pain, more suffering, and more rejection than any of us will ever know. He knows how weak and vulnerable we are. He sympathizes with us. Only Jesus is now our Advocate in Heaven sitting at the right hand of God, interceding for us (Hebrews 4:15; 7:25). Why wouldn't we want to take advantage of this inheritance?

Personal Reflection

I was so grateful when I first learned prayer is simply talking to God. It doesn't have to be long, formal, or boring. In fact, God doesn't want that either. He wants our heart, not empty ritual. He wants our heartfelt worship and praise. He wants our heartfelt gratitude and thanksgiving. He wants our heartfelt sorrow and confession of sin. He wants our heartfelt intercession for others. I find it helpful to write out my prayers because it helps me stay focused and pray in this way. But whether we sit or stand, lie down, or kneel, pray silently, out loud, or write out our prayers, God hears us and He answers us because Jesus gave us access to His throne.

A couple of examples from the Bible help us visualize the significance of this inheritance, one from the Old Testament and one from the New.

In the Old Testament, Isaiah was overcome with emotion when he had this vision of God's throne.

The Bible says:

> In the year that King Uzziah died, I saw the Lord seated on a throne, high and exalted, and the train of his robe filled the temple. Above him were seraphs, each with six wings: with two wings they covered their faces, with two they covered their feet, and with two they were flying. And they were calling to one another:
>
> "Holy, holy, holy is the Lord Almighty
>
> The whole earth is full of his glory."
>
> At the sound of their voices the doorposts and thresholds shook and the temple was filled with smoke. "Woe to me!" I cried. "I am ruined! For I am a man of unclean lips and I live among a people of unclean lips, and my eyes have seen the King, the Lord Almighty." (Isaiah 6:1-5)

Isaiah was a Jewish prophet seven hundred years before Christ, and here he is given a vision of God's throne room in Heaven. We can feel Isaiah's emotions as he pleads for God's mercy for himself and for his nation. And it gives us a tiny glimpse and insight into what it means to have the direct access to God that Jesus died to give us. This is our inheritance as His people. It was Isaiah's privilege to preview it and write about it, and it is ours to take advantage of thousands of years later.

In the New Testament, the Apostle John also had a vision of God's throne room after Jesus had ascended back to Heaven.

The Bible says:

> After this I looked and there before me was a door standing open in heaven. And the voice I had first heard speaking to me like a trumpet said, "Come up here, and I will show you what must take place after this." At once I was in the Spirit, and there before me was a throne in heaven with someone sitting on it. And the one who sat there had the appearance of jasper and carnelian. A rainbow resembling an emerald encircled the throne. Surrounding the throne were twenty-four other thrones, and seated on them were twenty-four elders.

John goes on to describe these elders and four living creatures in the center of the throne.

> Day and night the four living creatures never stopped saying:
>
> "Holy, holy, holy is the Lord God Almighty,
>
> Who was, and is, and is to come."
>
> And the twenty-four elders fell down before Him and laid their crowns before His throne saying:
>
> "You are worthy, our Lord and God,
>
> to receive glory and honor and power,
>
> for you created all things,
>
> and by your will they were created
>
> and have their being." (taken from Revelation 4:1-11)

This is our inheritance as believers in Jesus Christ. He has opened the door to the throne room of God, and we have direct access to Him. Isaiah and John had the vision but we have the reality.

Why would we ever want to miss out of this incredible inheritance?

Personal Thoughts and Study Guide

1. What has been your experience with prayer?

2. How would you define prayer and the value of this inheritance to you personally?

3. What motivates you to pray for those you love and the issues you care about?

4. How will Paul's example help you pray more effectively for yourself, your family, your church?

5. Define these terms from your own experience and how you want to move forward in each:

Spiritual wisdom and understanding

Living a life worthy of the Lord

Bearing fruit in every good work

Growing in knowledge of Him

Strengthened with His power

Qualified to share in the inheritance

Rescued from darkness

Redemption and forgiveness of sins

Remembering all Jesus died to give you

Make It Your Own

Which Bible verse on prayer will you memorize to help someone else know the importance of this inheritance? Write it down so you remember it.

Hymn:

What a Friend We Have in Jesus
by Joseph M. Scriven

What a friend we have in Jesus,
All our sins and griefs to bear!
What a privilege to carry
Everything to God in prayer!
Oh, what peace we often forfeit,
Oh, what needless pain we bear,
All because we do not carry
Everything to God in prayer!

Chapter 3

Eternal Security

*I*s there any word we hear more today than the word *security*? It comes with many different descriptions: personal security, homeland security, job security, financial security, retirement security, just to name a few, but the most important security we should be concerned with is our eternal security. Jesus has made it possible for every single human being to have this important assurance of where we will be after this life is over and all the other security issues we concern ourselves with are no longer necessary. But how do we have that assurance? Believers in Colossae were wondering the same thing because these false teachers were causing them to doubt their security in Christ.

In this next section of his letter, Paul makes it abundantly clear our eternal security is based on the supremacy of Jesus Christ. It is based on who He is. It is based on His rightful, ultimate, and final position of power and authority.

Here is our inheritance: Believers are safe in the presence of God forever because of who Jesus is. Believers have eternal security because of the supremacy of Jesus Christ.

The Bible says Paul describes Jesus' supremacy this way:

> He is the image of the invisible God, the firstborn over all
> creation. For by him all things were created: things in heaven
> and on earth, visible and invisible, whether thrones or powers
> or rulers or authorities; all things were created by him and
> for him. He is before all things, and in him all things hold
> together. And he is the head of the body, the church; he is
> the beginning and the firstborn from among the dead, so that
> in everything he might have the supremacy. For God was
> pleased to have all his fullness dwell in him, and through him
> to reconcile to himself all things, whether things on earth or
> things in heaven, by making peace with his blood, shed on
> the cross. Once you were alienated from God and enemies
> in your minds because of your evil behavior. But now he has
> reconciled you by Christ's physical body through death to
> present you holy in his sight, without blemish and free from
> accusation—if you continue in your faith, established and
> firm, not moved from the hope held out in the gospel. This
> is the gospel that you heard and that has been proclaimed
> to every creature under heaven, and of which I, Paul, have
> become a servant. (Colossians 1:15-23)

Knowing Our Inheritance

The tendency today is to dethrone Jesus. We want to make
Him into our image instead of conforming to His image. We don't
want to be restrained in our behavior. We don't want to deny our
desires and pleasures. We want the freedom to do and be what we
want to do and be while at the same time recognizing Jesus has
some role to play in our lives—just not to control them. This is
always the foundation for any false teaching within the church,
whether in Paul's day or our own. Denying Jesus His rightful place
of supremacy makes a mockery of the cross, debunks our faith
and the hope we have of salvation and eternal life, and therefore
destroys the church. That's why Paul addresses Jesus' position of
supremacy, His rightful authority, because without it, we are still
dead in our sins. In that condition, we have no hope for anything
but going to Hell when we die. Jesus' supremacy is the rock-solid

foundation of our faith. It is crucial we understand this great truth and the value of this inheritance for ourselves. Let's make sure we understand what Paul says about Jesus.

Paul lays it out like this:

Jesus is the image of the invisible God. In other words, Jesus is God.

Jesus is the firstborn over all creation, meaning He pre-existed all things, created all things, and is the sovereign ruler over all things and all people. Everything is created for Him, by Him, and through Him.

Jesus sustains all things and holds everything together.

Jesus is the head of the church—the body of believers around the world.

Jesus' resurrection guarantees our resurrection and proves His supremacy over all things, including life and death, Heaven and Hell.

God was pleased to have His fullness dwell in Jesus. God and Jesus are One and the same.

God was pleased to reconcile us to Himself through the blood of Jesus.

Through Jesus' physical death, we are presented to God, holy, without blemish, and free from accusation.

Jesus is the object of our faith and we are to stay established and firmly rooted in Him, for this is the gospel we have inherited and this is the gospel we are to proclaim.

This is a powerful message and a timeless legacy. The bottom line is we can only know God when we come face to face with Jesus Christ. He is all we need to have the security we are seeking.

Receiving Our Inheritance

Paul addresses this issue head on because people then needed this assurance just as people do today. But on what do we base this assurance? We can only base it on the Person, purpose, and provision of Jesus Christ. He alone is eternal. He alone is qualified through His life, death, resurrection, and ascension to resurrect us and allow us to share eternal life with Him. His supremacy over all things is our guarantee.

Bible verses to consider on eternal security:

We have this hope (Jesus) as an anchor for the soul, firm and secure. (Hebrews 6:19)

Your throne was established long ago; you are from all eternity. (Psalm 93:2)

Your word, O Lord, is eternal; it stands firm in the heavens. (Psalm 119:89)

Trust in the Lord forever, for the Lord, the Lord, is the Rock forever. (Isaiah 26:4)

For God so loved the world that he gave his one and only Son, that whoever believes in him shall not perish but have eternal life. (John 3:16)

Whoever believes in the Son has eternal life, but whoever rejects the Son will not see life for God's wrath remains on him. (John 3:36)

"I tell you the truth, whoever hears my word and believes him who sent me has eternal life and will not be condemned; he has crossed over from death to life." (John 5:24)

And this is the testimony: God has given us eternal life, and this life is in His Son. (1 John 5:11)

God is not a man that he should lie, nor a son of man, that he should change his mind. (Numbers 23:19)

Now to the King eternal, immortal, invisible, the only God, be honor and glory for ever and ever. Amen. (1 Timothy 1:16)

Living Our Inheritance

Our eternal security is guaranteed by Jesus Christ Himself. This is the assurance we rest on. This is the unchanging truth we live by. This is the promised hope we look forward to. As believers nothing can change our status before God because nothing can ever undo the work Jesus accomplished for us on the cross. Our reservation is made in Heaven, and nothing will ever cancel it. Therefore, we can live in faith and not fear; conviction and confidence and not cowardice; hope and joy and not hopelessness and despair. We can have passion and purpose because we know what we believe, who we believe, and why we believe. We are totally committed to the unchanging truth of the eternal Word of God.

Personal Reflection

Every day the news brings more bad news: more terrorist attacks, more mass shootings, more threats of nuclear war and global conflict, more government scandals and exposed corruption, more natural disasters uprooting millions and costing billions, all of which create insecurity. In fact, never before have people felt so insecure, anxious, and fearful about life and their future. Jesus knew this day was coming. He prepared His followers for it in the first century so they could record His words for us to read in the twenty-first century. Time is running out for people of every nationality, language, culture, background, and spiritual experience to come to Jesus. He is sovereign over and yet available to each one of us. He is eternal and trustworthy and He will never change. We can know with full assurance He has our back.

Personal Thoughts and Study Guide

1. What are your thoughts on your own security after you die?

2. How would you summarize Paul's description of Jesus? How does this make you feel more secure?

3. What is most precious to you and what are you in most need of in the security Jesus offers?

4. Who or what are you most apt to trust for your security over Jesus? Why? What has been the result?

5. What are some additional thoughts on security from the following verses: Deuteronomy 33:12; Psalm 16:5-6; Psalm 112; Proverbs 14:26?

6. How will this inheritance of security in Christ make you trust Him more? What do you need to release to Him so you can?

7. How does knowing you have eternal security change your priorities and your outlook on life and death?

Make It Your Own

Which Bible verse on security will you commit to memory as your go-to verse when you feel insecure or to share with someone else when they do? Write it out to help you remember it.

Hymn:

All Hail the Power of Jesus' Name
by Edward Perronet

All hail the pow'r of Jesus' Name!
Let angels prostrate fall;
Bring forth the royal diadem,
And crown Him Lord of all!

Chapter 4

Fuel in the Tank

*W*hat drove Paul to be so concerned about these believers in Colossae whom he had never even met? What inspired him to write this letter to them? What motivated him to pray so earnestly for them to continue strong in their faith in spite of the opposition they were facing? And what made him so determined to teach them that he risked his life for it? After all, Paul was in prison for his faith. He could have simply quit preaching the gospel and been a free man. But instead he counts his life as nothing if he can't continue to preach and help people come to Jesus. There is only one answer to these questions. The Holy Spirit of God drove Paul. This is the inheritance we all receive as believers.

Here is our inheritance: The Holy Spirit of God lives in all believers to fuel our tank.

We have already learned (in Chapter 2) believers receive the Holy Spirit the moment they put their faith and trust in Jesus Christ and accept His offer of salvation from sin. And because God's Spirit is now in us, we can approach our holy God in prayer.

But now Paul teaches us by his example how much more the Holy Spirit does for us. The Holy Spirit actually provides the fuel we need to live our life as believers. Therefore, the Holy Spirit is our teacher, motivator, inspiration, companion, challenger, counselor, corrector, comforter, encourager, strengthener, stress-reliever, peace-giver, and the energy behind all we do as followers of Jesus Christ.

The Holy Spirit is Christ living in us to accomplish His purpose through us. So the opposite is also true. Without the Holy Spirit, our actions might be well-motivated and good in their own right, but in the end, they are self-serving and have no eternal value. Therefore, it is crucial we understand the role the Holy Spirit plays in our lives as believers. Paul demonstrates that well in this letter to the church in Colossae.

The Bible says Paul wrote:

> Now I rejoice in what was suffered for you, and I fill up in my flesh what is still lacking in regard to Christ's afflictions, for the sake of his body, which is the church. I have become its servant by the commission God gave me to present to you the word of God in its fullness—the mystery that has been kept hidden for ages and generations, but is now disclosed to the saints. To them God has chosen to make known among the Gentiles the glorious riches of this mystery, which is Christ in you, the hope of glory. We proclaim him, admonishing and teaching everyone with all wisdom, so that we may present everyone perfect in Christ. To this end I labor, struggling with all his energy, which so powerfully works in me. (Colossians 1:24-29)

Knowing Our Inheritance

Paul's work for Christ is driven by the Holy Spirit. We could say Paul's tank is full. He has given his all to Jesus Christ, and as a result, Jesus has given Paul everything he needs to do the work. Every aspect of Paul's life is surrendered to Christ and for His church. Paul has gone from being super proud and protective of his Jewish heritage and looking down on everyone who doesn't have the same to wanting everyone to have what he has now. He has gone from being a rich and powerful Pharisee to becoming a lowly, imprisoned, and seemingly at-the-end-of-his-road servant. And yet we sense nothing but his joy, humility, gratitude, strength, determination, and absolute, unabashed love for Jesus Christ. Paul has abandoned his own life, ambitions, desires, and needs to fulfill His call on his life—to share God's message of salvation through the Jews to the Gentiles. This mystery that the good news of salvation is now available to everyone had been concealed for ages but is now revealed. Paul is God's man for the job, and he is fully aware none of this comes from him, but it is God's Spirit working in him.

Paul continues to tell this church in Colossae:

> I want you to know how much I am struggling for you and for those at Laodicea, and for all who have not met me personally. My purpose is that they may be encouraged in heart and united in love, so that they have the full riches of complete understanding, in order that they may know the mystery of God, namely, Christ, in whom are hidden all the treasures of wisdom and knowledge. I tell you this so that no one may deceive you by fine sounding arguments. For though I am absent from you in body, I am present with you in spirit and delight to see how orderly you are and how firm your faith in Christ is. (Colossians 2:1-5)

Paul's sole purpose and commitment in life is for as many people as possible to come to the same understanding of who Jesus Christ is, and of the inheritance we can have in Him. He doesn't want any false teaching to keep that from happening. It is Paul's intense desire for people to know Jesus as he knows Him and to have His Holy Spirit fill their tanks as the Holy Spirit continues to fill his.

Receiving Our Inheritance

This same Holy Spirit is ours when we belong to Jesus Christ, but we need to understand how the Holy Spirit works. He moves in when we receive Christ. He comes into our very being. He takes up residence within us. But from then on it is our choice as to how much of us He has. So it is not a question of how much of the Holy Spirit we have but how much He has of us. Our tank can either be on reserve, a quarter full, half full or full. It's just like going to the gas station and fueling our car. Do we just want a little gas to go a little ways or a full tank to go a long way? And how much do we want to spend in terms of giving up ourselves and our own agenda to have what He wants to give us? Perhaps these verses will help answer those questions.

Bible verses to consider on the Holy Spirit:

> I will give you a new heart and put a new spirit in you; I will remove from you your heart of stone and give you a heart of flesh. And I will put my Spirit in you and move you to follow my decrees and be careful to keep my laws. (Ezekiel 36:26)

> "Not by might nor by power but by my Spirit," says the Lord Almighty. (Zechariah 4:6)

> "The Counselor, the Holy Spirit, whom the Father will send in my name, will teach you all things and remind you of everything I have said to you." (John 14:26)

> "When he, the Spirit of truth, comes, he will guide you into all truth." (John 16:13)

> "Receive the Holy Spirit." (John 20:23)

> "You will receive power when the Holy Spirit comes on you." (Acts 1:8)

> You, however, are controlled not by the sinful nature but by the Spirit, if the Spirit of God lives in you. And if anyone does not have the Spirit of Christ, he does not belong to Christ. (Romans 8:9)

> Do you not know that your body is a temple of the Holy Spirit, who is in you, whom you have received from God? You are not your own; you were bought at a price. Therefore honor God with your body. (1 Corinthians 6:19)

Now it is God who has made us for this very purpose (heaven) and has given us the Spirit as a deposit, guaranteeing what is to come. (2 Corinthians 5:5)

The fruit of the Spirit is love, joy, peace, patience, kindness, goodness, faithfulness, gentleness and self-control. (Galatians 5:22-23)

Having believed (the gospel), you were marked in him with a seal, the promised Holy Spirit, who is a deposit guaranteeing our inheritance until the redemption of those who are God's possession—to the praise of his glory. (Ephesians 1:13)

Do not get drunk on wine, which leads to debauchery. Instead, be filled with the Spirit. (Ephesians 5:18)

Living Our Inheritance

Why would we possibly want to live any other way when the Holy Spirit of Almighty God wants to make His residence in us to be our constant guide and companion through life? Why would we want any less of Him than He wants to give us? There is only one answer. Our pride gets in the way just like it did with Adam and Eve in the Garden of Eden. Satan tempted them to disobey God, and their determination to have their own way cost them the relationship He wanted to have with them. Nothing has changed in the human heart. Only Jesus can change it. That's why He sent His Holy Spirit to live in us, because even if we wanted to, we could never live for Jesus without Jesus Himself living in us. This is the incredible inheritance He left us, and it becomes ours the moment we trust Him for salvation. Immediately, our life takes on a whole new meaning, which we will continue to explore. But the presence of God in us awakens our senses, sharpens our minds, quickens our hearts, and gives us new energy, new focus, and new purpose because we are in alignment with God.

This was Paul's inheritance and it can be ours as well.

Personal Reflection

I love living with the Holy Spirit because it's His job to keep me close to Jesus. He activates my conscience and makes me aware of when I am making a bad choice or taking a wrong turn or about to say something offensive or already have. He holds me back or pushes me forward according to God's will in my life. My job is to listen to His still small voice and obey. When I don't, He causes me to repent and turn around because He has given me a deep desire — no, need — to be right with Him. Everything else in my life becomes secondary to knowing I am in sync with God and therefore pleasing to Him. Could Jesus have left us with a better inheritance than the Holy Spirit living in us making our heart His home?

Personal Thoughts and Study Guide

1. What is the energy that is working so powerfully in Paul? How would you describe the "fuel in his tank"?

2. Why was Paul suffering, what was the mystery he revealed, and what role did the Holy Spirit play in his life?

3. How do you relate the Holy Spirit to God the Father and God the Son? Describe the role of each.

4. Describe your relationship with the Holy Spirit and the value of this inheritance in your own life.

5. How much of you does the Holy Spirit have now and how much of you do you want Him to have? Are you willing to give it to Him?

6. What will you ask the Holy Spirit to help you with to be closer to Jesus?

7. What do you need to give up of yourself to help you do that?

8. What are you particularly thankful to the Holy Spirit for?

Make It Your Own

Which Bible verse on the Holy Spirit will you memorize and make your go-to verse when you find yourself denying His rightful place in your life? Write it down so you remember it.

Hymn:

Spirit Divine
by Andrew Reed

Spirit divine, inspire our prayer,
And make our hearts your home;
Descend with all your gracious power;
Come, Holy Spirit, come!

Chapter 5

Strength for the Journey

*H*as God ever asked you to do something that seemed so impossible to you that you laughed inside yourself even at the possibility? Then when you did it, you wondered how you did it before realizing it wasn't you at all but God working in you to accomplish His own purpose, and you were just the privileged bystander!

Part of the Holy Spirit's work in us is to give us the strength we need to accomplish the work God calls us to do. We can see how this works in Paul's life. At this stage, he had exhausted all his own resources. He had given up everything he owned and the rights to his own life to follow Jesus and proclaim His gospel of salvation to the known world. By this time Paul had been on three missionary journeys to accomplish that purpose. According to his own record, he had experienced hardship of every kind, starvation, exposure to the elements, floggings, beatings, stoning, shipwrecks, robberies, prison, and the daily pressure of concern for the churches he had begun (2 Corinthians 11:23-29). He had been hated by his own people, the Jews, as well as Gentiles and the false teachers he was determined to expose. If that wasn't enough, Paul suffered from some sort of chronic pain that he begged Jesus three different times to remove, and Jesus said "no." Yet Paul kept going. He stayed strong in the midst of adversity, continued hardship, opposition, and much pain and suffering.

We never know what God is going to ask us to do, but as believers we can have the same strength Paul had.

Here is our inheritance: Jesus' strength is available to all believers.

The Holy Spirit gives us the power and strength to be more like Jesus. In this section of his letter to the church in Colossae, Paul shares the strength he received for the task he was given and tells us how we can have the same.

The Bible says Paul wrote:

> So then, just as you received Christ Jesus as Lord, continue to live in him, rooted and built up in him, strengthened in the faith as you were taught, and overflowing with thankfulness. See to it that no one takes you captive through hollow and deceptive philosophy, which depends on human tradition and the basic principles of this world rather than on Christ. For in Christ all the fullness of the Deity lives in bodily form, and you have been given fullness in Christ, who is the head over every power and authority. In him you were also circumcised, in the putting off of the sinful nature, not with a circumcision done by the hands of men but with the circumcision done by Christ, having been buried with him in baptism and raised with him through your faith in the power of God, who raised him from the dead. (Colossians 2:6-12)

Knowing Our Inheritance

Paul outlines his secret for tapping into Jesus' strength. First, we must understand receiving Jesus as our Savior is a one-time event, but to "continue" with Jesus, as Paul stresses here, is a lifetime event. It is a process called sanctification which begins when the Holy Spirit takes up residence in us at the time of our conversion. His work is to make us more like Jesus. This is a lifelong process which Paul describes as being "rooted and built up" in Him. Just as plants can't grow unless they have deep roots drawing strength from the soil, we can't grow strong in our faith unless our roots are deep in Christ and watered regularly. Only then can we become "built up" in Him which always makes us more thankful as Paul recommends here.

Knowing we belong to Jesus and we are continuing in Jesus also makes us more discerning of the "hollow and deceptive" teachings that have threatened the church since its inception. We are committed to His supremacy and sovereignty over all things and not willing to abdicate His throne to anyone or anything. Therefore, we are aware of and can make the distinction between human traditions and the basic principles of this world that replace or distract us from Christ. He is number one in our life and faith. We have experienced the "fullness of His Deity." We believe He is God in the flesh and the head over every power and authority.

Paul uses circumcision as the sign of this ownership. God gave circumcision to the Israelites as the sign they were His chosen people. This set them apart from all the pagan people around them. Now Paul uses this analogy to indicate believers have been cut to the heart by Jesus Christ. This "surgery" puts off our sinful nature. In other words, our desire to please Him replaces our desire to sin. There is no other way for this to be accomplished except by His presence living in us and convicting us of sin. This power to change is only available when we "die" to ourselves and our own lives and are "raised with Him through our faith in the power of God, who raised Him from the dead."

We can see the progression in Paul's thinking and our ability to draw on this inheritance of Jesus' strength. Paraphrasing the text will help us.

Receive Christ.

Continue in Christ.

Be firmly rooted and built up in Christ.

Strengthen your faith with what you have been taught about Christ.

Overflow with thankfulness to Christ.

Know Christ and His teachings so you are not deceived by counterfeits.

Keep Christ number one.

Remember Christ is God in human form.

Acknowledge Christ as head over every power and authority.

Live like you belong to Christ.

You were buried with Christ in baptism—when you identified with Him—and raised with Christ—from old life of sin—by the same power that raised Him from the dead.

Receiving Our Inheritance

This is the strength available to us as believers. It is the strength of Almighty God who gave His strength to Jesus as His incarnate Son and is now passing down to us. It begs the question, why do we try so hard to be strong by ourselves? Why do we work so hard at making our bodies strong, our emotions strong, and our minds strong when all are secondary to making our faith in Him strong? Our bodies break down, our emotions break down, and our minds can break down when our journey through life becomes too difficult, but a deeply rooted faith in Jesus Christ can weather any storm because He is taking the brunt of it and protecting and guiding us through it. The bonus is we always come through stronger than we were before.

Bible verses to consider on God's strength:

The Lord is my strength and my song; he has become my salvation. (Exodus 15:2)

The eternal God is your refuge, and underneath are the everlasting arms. (Deuteronomy 33:27)

It is God who arms me with strength and makes my way perfect. (2 Samuel 22:33)

The joy of the Lord is your strength. (Nehemiah 8:10)

The Lord is my strength and my shield; my heart trusts in him, and I am helped. (Psalm 28:7)

God is our refuge and strength, an ever-present help in trouble. (Psalm 46:1)

The Lord is with me; he is my helper. (Psalm 118:7)

Those who hope in the Lord will renew their strength. They will soar on wings of eagles; they will run and not grow weary, they will walk and not be faint. (Isaiah 40:31)

The foolishness of God is wiser than man's wisdom and the weakness of God is stronger than man's strength. (1 Corinthians 1:25)

I can do everything through Him who gives me strength. (Philippians 4:13)

If anyone serves, he should do it with the strength God provides, so that in all things God may be praised through Jesus Christ. (1 Peter 4:11)

"My grace is sufficient for you, for my power is made perfect in weakness." (2 Corinthians 12:8)

Living Our Inheritance

How can we fully comprehend and appreciate the strength Jesus offers us as His followers? How do we draw on His strength in our own lives? The answer is found in His example. Think of it. The same strength that enabled Jesus to triumph in His life is available to help us triumph in ours. We can draw on His physical, mental, emotional, and spiritual strength as His followers. Throughout His thirty-three years as a human being with our same limitations, He showed us by example how to overcome poverty, rejection, physical, mental, emotional, and spiritual abuse and the most brutal and agonizing death in human history. Although He was fully God, He was also fully man and as such suffered as we would under the same circumstances. Nothing was made easier for Him. In fact, Jesus' suffering was even more brutal than anything we will ever experience because in the end, even His Father had to turn away from Him because of our sin. Jesus had willingly taken our sins upon Himself to pay the debt we owed but could never pay, and until this work was completed, our holy and perfect God could not look on His now, sin-bearing Son. That is why Jesus' words from the cross were not the words of a helpless victim but of a victorious conqueror. His words were not a whimper of defeat but a shout of triumph. "It is finished" announced to the world then and now that Jesus completed the work His Father sent Him to do.

The sheer strength of Jesus' mind and body to accomplish this work for us is our inheritance to put to use in our lives. His life, documented in the four Gospels, is our example to follow.

We can follow His example to obey God.

We can follow His example to study and apply His Word.

We can follow His example to be in the world but not of the world.

We can follow His example to pray.

We can follow His example to surround ourselves with like-minded believers.

We can follow His example to share His strength in us with others.

We can follow His example to pass on the truth of the gospel so His strength reproduces itself in our world and the world becomes a better place.

We can follow His example and know whatever we face in this life pales in comparison to the glory that awaits us in Heaven.

Personal Reflection

Every day we wake up to new circumstances and a new set of challenges. Some days are easier than others but one thing is always the same: we choose how we are going to respond to the ups and downs in life; we can choose to be victims or we can choose to be overcomers. Once again Jesus gives us the example. He said, "In this world you will have trouble. But take heart! I have overcome the world" (John 16:33). When we align ourselves with Him, He gives us the strength to overcome the difficult and painful situations we face. Many years ago, I made a vow to Him not to let another day go by without depending on His strength to help me through. We live in a fallen world and are never spared painful times in life, but He keeps His promises. He is faithful to His people. We can count on Him. We are given His strength for the journey. Another amazing inheritance!

Personal Thoughts and Study Guide

1. Why was Paul so concerned about this church in Colossae?

2. What hollow and deceptive philosophies threaten the church today?

3. What can you learn and apply from the strength Paul demonstrated in these circumstances?

4. Describe a difficult situation you are facing and how you are dealing with it.

5. Who or what are you depending on for your strength instead of the strength Jesus provides through His Holy Spirit? How has it been working for you? What needs to change for you to depend more on Him?

6. What does it mean for you to keep Christ number one?

7. What does it mean for you to "continue on" in Christ?

8. What does it mean for you to be buried with Christ in baptism and raised again?

9. How will you thank God for this incredible inheritance?

Make It Your Own

Which Bible verse on God's strength will you commit to memory as your go-to verse when you need strength for your journey? Write it down to help you remember it.

Hymn:

The Solid Rock
by Edward Mote

My hope is built on nothing less than Jesus' blood and righteousness;
I dare not trust the sweetest frame,
But wholly lean on Jesus' name.
On Christ, the solid rock I stand;
All other ground is sinking sand;
All other ground is sinking sand.

Chapter 6

Forgiveness

orgiveness is one of the most powerful words in any language on earth and certainly one of the most difficult to give or to receive. Yet without it, either the one who needs to forgive or the one who needs forgiveness is living in bondage. Bondage to sin; bondage to guilt and shame; bondage to insecurity and inferiority; bondage to anger, frustration, and fear; bondage to resentment and bitterness; bondage to depression and despair; and most certainly, bondage to death. On the other hand, forgiveness offers a fresh start, a new beginning, a different course. Forgiveness brings new life, new hope, new vision, and a new future.

Here is our inheritance: Jesus made it possible for us to receive forgiveness and for us to forgive others.

Paul never got over the power of God's forgiveness in his own life. It governed his life going forward from the time of his conversion. Now in his letter to the church in Colossae, he helps believers then and now realize how essential forgiveness is, both to receive and then to pass on. Paul helps us see the value of this inheritance in our own lives.

The Bible says Paul said:

> When you were dead in your sins and in the uncircumcision of your sinful nature, God made you alive with Christ. He forgave us all our sins, having canceled the written code, with its regulations, that was against us and that stood opposed to us; he took it away, nailing it to the cross. And having disarmed the powers and authorities, he made a public spectacle of them, triumphing over them by the cross. (Colossians 2:13-15)

Knowing Our Inheritance

Paul makes our condition without Christ graphically clear. We are dead! Just as dead as a corpse in the morgue. Even though we are physically alive, we are spiritually dead and therefore doomed to the limits of our physical life. Once again Paul uses circumcision to symbolize what takes place to bring us this new life. In the Old Testament, we know God had given circumcision to the Israelites to separate them from the pagan people around them and to prove they belonged to Him. In the New Testament, Jesus used it to symbolize the cutting away of anything in a believer's heart that separates us from Him. His death on the cross provides the bridge for us to cross over from spiritual death to spiritual life. The cross was God's provision for us to be forgiven for our sins. The cross made the written code, or the Old Testament Law which governed the lives of the people, obsolete because no one could keep it. Therefore no one could be saved by it. But Jesus met all the requirements of the law, and when we give ourselves to Him, His righteousness becomes our righteousness. This was the amazing work He accomplished for us on the cross. This is why His first words were, "Father, forgive them because they know not what they do" (Luke 23:34). And later He said, "It is finished!" (John 19:30). This act of forgiveness, generated by God the Father and executed by Jesus, the Son, changed the world forever. The power of His forgiveness opened Heaven to all believers. Our sins were nailed to the cross with His tortured body and buried with Him. But unlike His glorious body that rose from the grave three days later, our sins remain there, never to rise again. As Paul says in this passage, sin was "disarmed" that day, and the hold sin had had over us since Adam and Eve was broken forever.

Receiving Our Inheritance

When we come to the cross and accept Jesus' sacrifice on our behalf, we are immediately forgiven just as assuredly as the thief who died on the cross next to Him. In his pitiful and desperate state, the thief cried out to Jesus and asked Him to please remember him when he came into His paradise. This man had no other information except what he was witnessing as he was hanging there alongside Jesus. But that was enough to convince him of Jesus' position and favor with God, so he flung himself at His mercy. Jesus responded with these often-quoted words that have comforted countless billions ever since, "Today, you will be with me in paradise!" (Luke 23:43). When we bow our heads and surrender our hearts to Jesus Christ, we no longer stand condemned. We are forgiven. That is the powerful reality of the cross. That is our inheritance as believers. It only stands to reason we want to pass forgiveness on.

Later in this letter Paul says:

> Bear with each other and forgive whatever grievances you may have against one another. Forgive as the Lord forgave you. (Colossians 3:13)

Living Our Inheritance

Paul makes it clear forgiveness is not just a suggestion or a good idea but it's a command. We are commanded to forgive because we have received God's forgiveness. But we can only forgive others when we fully comprehend what our forgiveness costs God both as the Father and as the Son.

God created us to experience His goodness and His presence forever. He created us to live in peace and harmony. But sin made that impossible.

Sin violated God's nature and holiness.

Sin separates us from God because sin and holiness are not compatible.

Sin marred God's creation and denies us the goodness He intended for us.

Sin creates an abyss we cannot cross and a problem we cannot fix.

Sin incurs God's just wrath and has to be appeased or satisfied for us to be reconciled to God.

Sin requires a Savior.

In His mercy and great love for us, God sent His Son.

Jesus fulfilled His Father's will and came to rescue us from this separated and condemned state.

Jesus left the presence of His Father and the glory of Heaven.

Jesus came to earth as one of us to be the necessary sacrifice that would save us from our sin.

Jesus' death was the ONLY sacrifice God would accept.

Jesus' death was the ONLY way to appease God's justified wrath over sin.

Forgiveness is not easy. Forgiveness is always costly. But that is what makes it so precious and also what makes it so necessary.

Perhaps these thoughts and additional Bible verses will help our understanding and therefore our ability both to receive and then pass on this vitally important inheritance.

Thoughts on Forgiveness

Forgiveness sets us free to live and to love.

Forgiveness restores our relationship with God and others.

Forgiveness follows Jesus' example and obeys His command to do the same.

Forgiveness draws others to Jesus.

Forgiveness is good for our body, mind, and soul.

Forgiveness gives us peace.

Bible verses to consider on forgiveness:

Then I acknowledged my sin to you and did not cover up my iniquity. I said, "I will confess my transgressions to the Lord" and you forgave the guilt of my sin. (Psalm 32:5)

Be kind and compassionate to one another, forgiving each other, just as in Christ God forgave you. (Ephesians 4:32)

Who can discern his errors? Forgive my hidden faults. (Psalm 19:12)

Forgive us our debts as we also have forgiven our debtors. (Matthew 6:12)

For if you forgive men when they sin against you, your heavenly Father will also forgive you. But if you do not forgiven men their sins, your Father will not forgive your sins. (Matthew 6:14-15)

Then Peter came to Jesus and asked, "Lord, how many times shall I forgive my brother when he sins against me? Up to seven times?" Jesus answered, "I tell you, not seven times, but seventy-seven times." (Matthew 18:21-22)

If we confess our sins, he is faithful and just and will forgive us our sins. (1 John 1:9)

If you, O Lord, kept a record of sins, O Lord, who could stand? But with you there is forgiveness, therefore you are feared. (Psalm 130:4)

All the prophets testify about him that everyone who believes in him receives forgiveness of sins through his name. (Acts 10:43)

In him we have redemption through his blood, the forgiveness of sins, in accordance with the riches of God's grace that he lavished on us with all wisdom and understanding. (Ephesians 1:7)

In fact, the law requires that nearly everything be cleansed with blood, and without the shedding of blood there is no forgiveness. (Hebrews 9:22)

God established animal sacrifices in the Old Testament to point to the one, final, and complete sacrifice Jesus Christ would make for the sins of the world in the New Testament. He is "the Lamb of God that takes away the sin of the world" that John the Baptist came to announce and Jesus came to fulfill. (John 1:29)

All we can do in response is fall down before Him and thank Him for this incredible gift and awesome inheritance that benefits us first, and then is ours to pass on.

Personal Reflection

One of the greatest moments in my life was when I realized how much I needed God's forgiveness. I had carried a lot of baggage and was actually in bondage because of anger and bitterness toward my father's lack of involvement in my life. But the moment I recognized this as sin and confessed it before God, that anger and bitterness were gone and in their place was a love for my dad I had never experienced. This gave me the privilege of participating in and witnessing his spiritual conversion to Christ four months before he died.

This experience taught me that only when I know and believe God has forgiven me, am I able to obey Jesus' command to forgive someone else. It taught me the Biblical definition of forgiveness runs far deeper than the world's definition. The Biblical definition involves the very heart of God. It stems from His eternal love for us that sent His Son into the world to save us from our sin so we could be forgiven. God's forgiveness is binding and has eternal consequences. The world's definition is superficial, often dependent on the circumstances, and is not binding.

What an inheritance God has given us at the cost of His Son, and yet His Son is sitting at His right hand today looking forward to spending eternity with us.

Personal Thoughts and Study Guide

1. If you have not been to the cross to receive God's forgiveness through the blood Jesus shed for you on the cross, what is keeping you from receiving this most valuable inheritance?

2. If you have, how did that event reset your life, your way of living, and your ability to forgive others?

3. According to Paul, why are we commanded to forgive?

4. Describe a particularly difficult relationship or event that required your forgiveness.

5. What was the result for you? What was the result for the other person or people involved?

6. Is there someone you are withholding forgiveness from because you feel totally justified in not forgiving them?

7. What if God had felt that way toward you? What would your life be like if He did?

8. What do you need to forgive in yourself?

9. How do you see God's forgiveness being different than the way the world system, apart from God, describes forgiveness?

10. What will change in your thinking about forgiveness because of this chapter? How will you show God your gratitude for this inheritance?

Make It Your Own

Which Bible verse on forgiveness will you memorize and claim for yourself? Write it out to help you remember it.

Hymn:

Search Me, O God
by J. Edwin Orr

Search me, O God, and know my heart today,
Try me, O Savior, know my thoughts, I pray;
See if there be some wicked way in me;
Cleanse me from every sin, and set me free.

Chapter 7

Freedom to Live

*J*esus didn't leave the glory of Heaven and come down here to make life miserable for us. He didn't come to make our life more difficult. He didn't come to flaunt His power and control over us. He didn't come to be a harsh taskmaster, and He certainly didn't come to make us puppets. Jesus came to set us free from all the work, rules, and regulations we think we have to do and follow in order to be right with God. Jesus came to make our life better, freer, more satisfying, and fulfilling. Jesus came to make our life what God intended it to be in the first place.

In this section of his letter to the church in Colossae, Paul addresses this matter of being free of the law because these false teachers were teaching the importance of continuing to adhere to some Old Testament laws that were now obsolete or fulfilled by Jesus Christ. They were also enticing these believers into other forms of spirituality. Paul warns against both. Rituals and traditions may have a place, but they are not essential to salvation and therefore can be misleading. Other forms of spirituality deny the purity of the gospel. Both threaten the inheritance Jesus wants us to enjoy.

Here is our inheritance: Jesus freed us from unessential rules, rituals, and "extra stuff" so we can have a personal and authentic relationship with Him.

Once again, Paul helps us zero in on what really matters and therefore should remain our primary focus.

The Bible says Paul said:

> Therefore do not let anyone judge you by what you eat or drink, or with regard to a religious festival, a New Moon festival or a Sabbath day. These were a shadow of the things to come; the reality, however, is found in Christ. Do not let anyone who delights in false humility and the worship of angels disqualify you for the prize. Such a person goes into great detail about what he has seen, and his unspiritual mind puffs him up with idle notions. He has lost connection to the Head, from whom the whole body, supported and held together by its ligaments and sinews, grows as God causes it to grow. (Colossians 2:16-19)

Knowing Our Inheritance

In the Old Testament, God established the ceremonial law to govern how the Israelites worshipped Him. This included certain dietary rules to protect them and keep them growing as a nation. It was essential they followed these rules for their survival. God also established certain feast days and festivals to train them in their worship. These special days had specific purpose and pointed forward to Jesus Christ. So like Paul says here, "These were a shadow of things to come because the reality is found in Christ." Everything God commanded the Israelites to do in the Old Testament had meaning and pointed to Jesus Christ in the New Testament. It is a powerful example of how all sixty-six books of the Bible fit together to teach us God's plan and purpose—past, present, and future. Jesus set a new course for the human race. He set a new course for believers by establishing His church. He set a new course for believers to have an authentic, personal, and uncluttered relationship with Him. He set a new course for worship, and He set a new course to free us from the unnecessary burdens we put on ourselves in the name of worship. Paul also warns the church then and us today not to get sidetracked by fake pastors who are more into themselves and their own agendas than they are with the true gospel and the inerrancy of Scripture. We are to obey the first commandment which says, "Thou shalt have no other gods but me" (Exodus 20:3). And we are not to worship or pray to angels or saints or fall for any fake news that isn't fully supported and qualified in Scripture.

Once again, Jesus divides history. Paul reaffirms that in this passage and proves Jesus died to free us from such error.

The Bible says Paul continues:

> Since you died with Christ to the basic principles of this world, why, as though you still belonged to it, do you submit to its rules: "Do not handle! Do not taste! Do not touch!"? These are all destined to perish with use, because they are based on human commands and teachings. Such regulations indeed have an appearance of wisdom, with their self-imposed worship, their false humility and their harsh treatment of the body, but they lack any value in restraining sensual indulgence. (Colossians 2:20-23)

These false teachers refused to accept the fact that Jesus had canceled the ceremonial law. They refused to accept that Jesus' death changed history going forward. They used their influence to appear wise by making their own rules. They set themselves up to look pious and holy, but their humility was false, their worship was worthless, and their self-imposed physical abuse to control their sinful desires had failed.

The cross made it clear what God required to be right with Him and relieved mankind of the responsibility to add anything else. This is the freedom He offers. What a wonderful inheritance for us to receive!

Receiving Our Inheritance

Jesus not only divides history, He divides our lives into a definite "before and after" picture. Before we come to Him and are safe for all eternity because of Him, we belong to the world system apart from God. We are vulnerable to all its flaws and philosophies. We are subjects in its kingdom. But Jesus ushered in a new kingdom, and when we bow to Him and He becomes Lord over our life, we move from the world's kingdom into His kingdom. We are no longer the world's subjects, we are His subjects. Even though we still live in the world, it is not our permanent address. In fact, we are actually aliens and strangers because we now belong to Jesus Christ, and therefore we belong to His kingdom (1 Peter 2:11). This transition occurred when we "died" to our old way of living and came to life in Him.

The "before and after" picture makes us appreciate our freedom in Christ and give God the glory for it. It looks something like this:

Before, we were dead in our sins

Before, we were responsible for the debt our sin incurred.

Before, we were held hostage by our sin and in bondage because of our sin.

Before, we were helpless to help ourselves get out of our sin.

Before, we were subject to the ways of the world that fed our sin.

Before, our conscience and senses were dulled and we denied our sin.

Before, part of us loved our sin.

Before, we had no ability to give up our sin.

Before, we stand condemned and destined to Hell because of our sin.

And before, we thought we had to work our way out of our sin.

But now, look at the "after" picture:

After, we are made alive in Christ.

After, we are declared "debt-free"!

After, we no longer have to be hostages or in bondage to sin.

After, we have God's power in us to help us not sin.

After, we are wise to the temptations of the world and are equipped to avoid them.

After, our conscience and senses come alive and alert us to avoid sin.

After, we don't want to sin!

After, we have all God's resources available to us to help us not sin.

After, we stand forgiven in Christ and destined to Heaven.

And after, we can rest in that assurance.

Living Our Inheritance

No wonder Paul says stop living the way you used to. Stop trying to live in both kingdoms—you've moved! Stop succumbing to all the pressure to let unessential matters of our faith govern your life and your worship. Stop feeling guilty and responsible for your sins that Jesus has forgiven. Stop trying to add to what He has already done for you. Stay focused on Jesus and what He did for you on the cross and does for you every single day through the power of His Holy Spirit. Don't get caught up in a bunch of "human commands and teachings" because they will trip you up, confuse your thinking, and damage your witness as a believer.

Granted, some of these ideas and teachings can sound good and seem right, especially if the teacher is good looking and charismatic, but watch out! Any and all false teaching in the name of Jesus Christ will not stand. They are destined to perish. And stay away from any ideas of desecrating your beautiful body in the name of religion because Christ died for you. He loves you just as you are. Nothing can be added and nothing is necessary. In Him, you are perfect and complete. Cherish and cultivate your relationship with Him. Don't be led astray and think anything else is required. Some teachers may try and convince you there is or that He's not enough, but don't be fooled! Jesus came to set you free from such thinking, so be free!

Bible verses to consider on this freedom:

The Lord sets prisoners free. (Psalm 146:7)

The truth will set you free. (John 8:32)

You have been set free from sin. (Romans 6:18)

(Christ) has freed us from our sins by His blood. (Revelation 1:5)

Where the Spirit of the Lord is, there is freedom. (2 Corinthians 3:17)

You were called to be free but do not use your freedom to indulge the sinful nature. (Galatians 5:13)

Live as free men but do not use your freedom as a cover-up for evil; live as servants for God. (1 Peter 2:16)

Turn to the Lord ... and to our God, for he will freely pardon. (Isaiah 55:7)

We are justified freely by his grace through the redemption that came through Christ Jesus. (Romans 3:24)

To the praise of his glorious grace which he has freely given us in the One he loves. (Ephesians 1:6)

Freely you have received, freely give. (Matthew 10:8)

So if the Son sets you free, you will be free indeed. (John 8:36)

Personal Reflection

Sin is a terrible enemy. Freedom is a priceless gift. When I think about what it cost Jesus to set me free from the power and penalty of sin in my own life, I can't help but bow my head and my heart in gratitude for this amazing inheritance because He did it all. There is NOTHING I can add (or anyone or anything else can add) to what He has completed on my behalf. With that reality firmly cemented in my thinking, I can't help but love Him all the more. I can't help but want to please Him more. I can't help but want to sin less and serve Him more. I can't help but want to put my thoughts on paper and share them with you so you can share in this inheritance. There is enough of Jesus for all who come and put their faith and trust in Him.

Personal Thoughts and Study Guide

1. What was threatening the freedom of the believers in Colossae?

2. How do the same threats affect the church today?

3. What does the word *freedom* mean to you?

4. Have you received the inheritance of freedom Christ died to give you? If not, what is more important to you? If you have, what aspect of His freedom are you most thankful for?

5. What has He freed you from and what has He freed you to do as a result?

6. How has His freedom changed you and how has it changed the way you deal with people who don't yet have it?

7. What other "stuff" are you drawn to or hanging on to that could be stifling the freedom you have in Jesus?

8. What does your "before and after" picture look like? Write it out so you can thank Jesus for each "makeover."

Make It Your Own

Which Bible verse on the freedom Christ offers will you memorize and refer to when you are tempted to go back into bondage by a particular sin? Write it out to help you remember it.

Hymn:

Just as I Am, O Lamb of God
By Horace L. Hastings

Just as I am, without delay,
Now I come, now I come;
To Christ the true and living Way,
Now I come, now I come.
For pardon purchased on the tree,
For grace and mercy rich and free,
O Lamb of God, I come to Thee,
Now I come, now I come.

Chapter 8

Peace in the Present

$\mathcal{T}$he world is clamoring for peace. Nations are clamoring for peace. Cities are clamoring for peace. Schools are clamoring for peace. Families are clamoring for peace. Individuals are clamoring for peace. And yet peace is so elusive. One day things can seem peaceful on all these fronts. But the next day, the headlines warn of nuclear attack; wars and rumors of wars abound among the nations; crime erupts in our cities; protests continue in our schools; our families are in one crisis after another; and individuals are experiencing an all-time record of stress and anxiety. What is the answer? We know the answer is not in the United Nations; it's not in our government or political system; it's not in our city councils or school boards; it's not in drugs, alcohol, or medication to numb our senses. Genuine and lasting peace, peace that defies reason and circumstances, peace that wells up from deep within us when everything is in chaos around us, is only found in one source and that source is Jesus Christ. In His own words, He described the peace He offers before leaving this earth and returning to Heaven.

The Bible says Jesus said:

> Peace I leave with you; my peace I give you. I do not give to you as the world gives. Do not let your hearts be troubled and do not be afraid. (John 14:27)

Here is our inheritance: The world apart from God won't know peace until Jesus returns, but believers can have peace in the present.

God's peace is a priceless inheritance, and Paul spends this section of his letter to the church in Colossae telling believers how we can have it.

The Bible says Paul said:

> Since, then, you have been raised with Christ, set your hearts on things above, where Christ is seated at the right hand of God. Set your minds on things above, not on earthly things. For you died, and your life is now hidden with Christ in God. When Christ, who is your life, appears, then you also will appear with him in glory. Put to death, therefore, whatever belongs to your earthly nature: sexual immorality, impurity, lust, evil desires and greed, which is idolatry. Because of these, the wrath of God is coming. You used to walk in these ways, in the life you once lived. But now you must rid yourselves of all such things as these: anger, rage, malice, slander and filthy language from your lips. Do not lie to each other, since you have taken off your old self with its practices and have put on the new self, which is being renewed in knowledge in the image of its Creator. Here there is no Greek or Jew, circumcised or uncircumcised, barbarian, Scythian, slave or free, but Christ is all, and is in all. (Colossians 3:1-11)

Knowing Our Inheritance

Paul sets the stage for us to receive God's peace by reminding us of our "before and after" picture we saw in our last chapter. He makes it very clear we can live in a whole new atmosphere after we come to Christ. We don't need to be disturbed and distressed by the chaos around us. We don't need to be limited in our thinking or our ability to mature in our faith. The sky is literally the limit. Jesus is in Heaven, seated at the right hand of God praying for us (Hebrews 7:25). Why wouldn't we want to saturate our hearts and minds with just thinking about that?

We can't escape our earthly duties, of course, but since we have been "raised with Christ" like Paul says here, why aren't we more drawn to thinking about Him and our life from His perspective and less about this world we live in? Why would we ever want to go back to being the way we were when Paul says sexual immorality, impurity, lust, evil desires, and greed bring on God's wrath? We're all guilty of these sins in some degree, so Paul says "put them to death!" Kill these things that deprive you of time and space in your heart and mind for God.

Paul goes even further and says get rid of anger, rage, malice, slander and filthy language and while you're at it, stop lying! Set new goals for yourself! Look up and look forward to Jesus coming back in all His glory because when He does, we are going to be like Him. And who wants to be caught living in our old sinful ways when He comes? He has given us Himself and every resource at His disposal to help us grow away from our old way of living and grow into the new life He died to give us. Paul further adds there is no discrimination in Christ. Everyone who wants this new life has access to the inheritance He offers.

Paul continues to show us how to have God's peace. The Bible says:

> Therefore, as God's chosen people, holy and dearly loved, clothe yourselves with compassion, kindness, humility, gentleness and patience. Bear with each other and forgive whatever grievances you may have against one another. Forgive as the Lord forgave you. And over all these virtues put on love, which binds them all together in perfect unity. (Colossians 3:12-14)

Receiving Our Inheritance

We could describe this as a taking off and putting on. Paul has already told us what we have to take off—all those old sins and sinful desires we had before we came to Christ. But now we have to dress ourselves to look like Him. We have to consciously follow His example and act like Him. We must choose to be like Him. Why? Because we will never experience His peace that He is wanting us to have if we don't! We have to replace evil thoughts and emotions and actions with thoughts, emotions, and actions that represent Him to the world, draw us closer to Him, and lead to that peace we all want.

After all, how will we ever experience the peace of Jesus Christ if we aren't in sync with the way He calls us to live? Paul has set the stage for us to have this peace, so now let's see how we can claim this inheritance for ourselves.

The Bible says Paul continues:

> Let the peace of Christ rule in your hearts, since as members of one body you were called to peace. And be thankful. Let the word of Christ dwell in you richly as you teach and admonish one another with all wisdom, and as you sing psalms, hymns and spiritual songs with gratitude in your hearts to God. And whatever you do, whether in word or deed, do it all in the name of Jesus, giving thanks to God the Father through him. (Colossians 3:15-17)

In this passage Paul gives us the key to receiving this peace. Let's take it apart so we can understand it.

> Let Christ rule. This is active and ongoing. This means we have to consciously and consistently give Jesus the right to rule and overrule in our lives; the right to correct us and discipline us and redirect us; the right to our thoughts and emotions and desires and motives. Jesus wants all of us and we will only experience His peace when we give it to Him.

> Remember you are part of the body. All believers are part of the church universal (the Body of Christ). Therefore, it

is essential we work together and don't hurt the "body" by going back to our old way of life but we stay focused and obedient to Christ.

Be thankful. This is an all-inclusive thankfulness not a selective thankfulness. This is being thankful when we don't feel thankful. This is being thankful when we don't see anything to be thankful for. Being thankful goes deeper than our circumstances and feelings. Being thankful goes to the root of who we are in Christ and where we would be without Him. Thinking about Him always makes us thankful.

Immerse yourself in the Word of God. Just as vitamins strengthen our body, God's Word strengthens our soul, builds our faith, and keeps us on His path. When we deprive ourselves of this nourishment, we drift away from Him and expose ourselves to needless suffering and guilt.

Hold each other accountable. Surround yourself with some trusted Christian friends who will support you and pray for you. This is an absolute necessity for all of us as we strive to follow Christ.

Praise God with singing and prayer. Even if you can't sing, sing. God loves our praise and He loves our prayers even if we feel awkward or inadequate.

Do everything in the name of Jesus. This binds us to Him and makes us think about what we're doing and pray before doing it.

Living Our Inheritance

Paul is so practical in giving us these helps. He knows it is only when we discipline ourselves and become obedient to Christ's calling on our life that we will experience His peace. We will never experience this peace if we are compromising our faith and our relationship with Jesus by trying to live in both His kingdom and the world's kingdom. We will never have it if we neglect His Word.

We will never have it when we neglect spending time with Him in worship and prayer. But oh, the inheritance that is ours when we do.

Bible verses to consider on peace:

> The Lord turn his face toward you and give you peace. (Numbers 6:26)

> Turn from evil and do good; seek peace and pursue it. (Psalm 34:14)

> Righteousness and peace kiss each other. (Psalm 85:10)

> Great peace have they who love your law, and nothing can make them stumble. (Psalm 119:165)

> You will keep in perfect peace him whose mind is steadfast, because he trusts in you. (Isaiah 26:3)

> I have told you these things so that in me you may have peace. (John 16:33)

> Therefore, since we have been justified through faith, we have peace with God through our Lord Jesus Christ ... (Romans 5:1)

> For God is not a God of disorder but of peace. (1 Corinthians 15:33)

> The fruit of the Spirit is love, joy, peace, patience, kindness, goodness, faithfulness, gentleness and self-control. (Galatians 5:22-23)

> For he himself is our peace ... (Ephesians 2:14)

> And the peace of God, which transcends all understanding, will guard your hearts and your minds in Christ Jesus. (Philippians 4:7)

Now may the Lord of peace himself give you peace at all times and in every way. (2 Thessalonians 3:16)

Personal Reflection

I've heard it said peace is not the absence of conflict but the awareness of God's presence. His peace is a unique inheritance. It is only available for those who belong to Him. It is very different than the false peace the world offers. The world likes to tell us we can have peace by reading certain self-help books, or doing certain exercises, or taking certain classes, or going on a fabulous vacation, or just having some downtime. But while these things may help us cope and maybe make us feel better, they do not bring lasting peace. Even the temporary reprieve they bring is not real peace because God is not the source. God is the author of peace, and we need His Spirit living in us to access this great inheritance He has made available to us. I am so grateful for this gift in my life and for all the times I have leaned heavily on it to see me through.

Personal Thoughts and Study Guide

1. Describe a time when God's peace prevailed in very difficult circumstances in your life. Which verse listed, best describes the peace you experienced? Include it here.

2. What did it take for you to turn to Him instead of the false peace the world offers?

3. What sins did Paul name that have no place in the life of a believer?

4. What nagging sin in your life do you need to put to death once and for all?

5. What habit or attitude do you need to "take off" and what example of Jesus do you need to "put on" in its place?

6. How could your actions be hurting the church, the Body of Christ? What changes are you willing to make to bring peace to that situation?

7. Summarize Paul's teaching to the church in Colossae as to how to receive Christ's peace. Which one will you incorporate in your life today?

8. What do believers have to look forward to when Jesus returns?

9. In the meantime, how much time and focus do you give God's Word on a regular basis so you can enjoy His peace in the present?

Make It Your Own

Which Bible verse on peace will you memorize as your go-to verse when you need His peace or want to pass it on to someone else? Write it out to help you remember it.

Hymn:

It Is Well with My Soul
By Horatio G. Spafford

When peace, like a river, attendeth my way,
When sorrows like sea billows roll;
Whatever my lot, Thou hast taught me to say,
It is well, it is well with my soul.

Chapter 9

A Meaningful Life

*O*ne of the most basic needs we have as human beings is to feel needed and that our life matters or has a purpose. God created us that way. That's why He gave us ability and talent and ingenuity. We are not puppets. We are not carbon copies of each other. We were not mass-produced. We are, each one of us, created in His image as unique individuals. So part of God's plan when creating us different from the animal kingdom was to let us discover, explore, and cultivate the talents and abilities He imparted to us at conception. He delights in His children reaching the potential He gave them and allowing Him to use them for His glory. This gives our life the meaning, purpose, satisfaction, and fulfillment we all need and seek.

He also gave us order to help us achieve that goal. The opposite of order is chaos and confusion which brings discouragement and defeat. In this section of his letter to the church in Colossae, Paul helps us see how order in our families and other relationships and pursuits bring meaning and satisfaction to our life.

Here is our inheritance: Jesus gave us order to help us have a meaningful life.

Order is important in every aspect of life. Order keeps us focused and productive. Order provides a roadmap to reach our goals. Jesus demonstrated order when He fed thousands of people with a couple of fish and a few loaves of bread. He demonstrated order when He changed water to wine at a wedding feast in Cana. He demonstrated order when He obeyed His Father and went to the cross. Order makes us disciplined and responsible. Order is a good thing.

Paul begins this passage with order in the home.

The Bible says Paul said:

> Wives, submit to your husbands, as fitting to the Lord. Husbands, love your wives and do not be harsh with them. Children, obey your parents in everything, for this pleases the Lord. Fathers, do not embitter your children, or they will become discouraged. Slaves, obey your earthly masters in everything; and do it, not only when their eye is on you and to win their favor, but with sincerity of heart and reverence for the Lord. Whatever you do, work at it with all your heart, as working for the Lord, not for men, since you know you will receive an inheritance from the Lord as a reward. It is the Lord Christ you are serving. Anyone who does wrong will be repaid for his wrong, and there is no favoritism. Masters, provide your slaves with what is right and fair, because you know you also have a Master in heaven. (Colossians 3:18-4:1)

Knowing Our Inheritance

Paul addresses families first because the family is the basic unit of any society. Its success determines the success of cities, nations, and even civilizations. God instituted marriage in the Garden of Eden right after He created Adam and Eve. Marriage was the framework in which humans would multiply and ultimately fill up this beautiful earth He created for us and made our home. Adam and Eve were created equal as male and female (Genesis 1:27). But after the Fall in Genesis 3, the perfection they knew in the Garden was lost. Sin entered the human race. Life would no longer be perfect. It would be hard and challenging. They would have to work to survive. In His mercy, God assigned them different roles so they would. Adam would work the land and Eve would bear the children—both jobs extremely difficult. The land would be hard to cultivate. The children would be hard to bring into the world and hard to raise afterward. Sin had brought severe and lasting consequences. Those consequences continued on to Paul's day and they continue on to ours. Paul gave these instructions to families within the church to ease the burden and to help the family unit be successful. The family is a beautiful and sacred inheritance God is determined to protect.

Receiving Our Inheritance

Paul begins with wives, and says to "submit" to your husbands. And immediately we have a problem, because most women in the twenty-first century do not like that word. It conjures up all sorts of negative connotations and implies subservience or second place. But Paul does not intend it that way. It helps us understand his meaning when we put it with what he tells husbands—to love their wives and not be harsh with them. That makes submission more understandable because being loved and being treated with consideration and respect are foundational to a good marriage.

The word Paul uses here for love is not just human love but love that can only come from God. This love is called agape love and it is a sacrificial love. This is the love God has for His church. This kind of love encourages husbands and wives to work together rather than compete against each other. The word *submission* actually means to yield, comply, or accept, and who wouldn't yield, comply, or accept if they felt entirely loved and valued in this way? Paul encourages this order within the home because it creates an atmosphere where everyone knows how the family unit works. The love and respect the husband has for the wife invites her love and respect for him in return. The children are the beneficiaries. They know they have a formidable team as parents. This makes them feel secure and helps them reach their full potential. Paul also has an extra warning to the fathers not to embitter or provoke their children because this certainly undermines that goal.

Paul also addresses slaves and their masters because this was the culture he lived in. But we can apply his principles in our day as well, especially in the work place.

These key points will help all of us achieve more order and meaning in our life:

> No matter who you work for or what line of work you are in, keep Jesus your focus.

> Work to please Jesus.

> Work to bring Jesus honor and glory.

> Be sincere with other people.

> Show them Jesus in your actions and attitudes.

> Strive to do the right thing.

> Be fair with those you work for and those you work with.

> Always keep your eye on your inheritance. It's your reward.

Living Our Inheritance

God has a work for every believer to do. He does not waste the gifts and talents He has given us. Since we are made in His image, part of Himself is imparted deep within us. Therefore, we are creative, intelligent, and industrious. We are loving, caring, capable, and compassionate. We are generous, thoughtful, and resourceful. With God's help, there is nothing we can't accomplish. History has proven it. Paul tells us how we can maximize these gifts.

The Bible says Paul said:

> Devote yourselves to prayer, being watchful and thankful. And pray for us, too, that God may open a door for our message, so that we may proclaim the mystery of Christ, for which I am now in chains. Pray that I may proclaim it clearly, as I should. Be wise in the way you act toward outsiders; make the most of every opportunity. Let your conversation

be always full of grace, seasoned with salt, so that you may know how to answer everyone. (Colossians 4:2-6)

This is Paul's strategy for having meaning in his life and ministry. It helps us find the same in ours.

Pray about everything.

Watch for what God is doing.

Thank Him during the process.

Have friends who will pray with you and for you.

Be obedient and stay focused on what He calls you to do.

Use every opportunity to represent Jesus well.

Extend grace.

Always be armed with the Word of God and the Spirit of God.

This was the secret of Paul's life. This was what got him out of bed every morning and motivated him to keep putting his life on the line for Jesus Christ. This was the ultimate meaning, fulfillment, and satisfaction of his life. Even though he was in chains, we can still sense the joy and profound gratitude his commitment to Christ continued to give him.

Bible verses to consider for a having a meaningful life:

Be joyful always; pray continuously; give thanks in all circumstances, for this is Christ's will for you in Christ Jesus. (1 Thessalonians 5:16)

The fear of the Lord is the beginning of knowledge, but fools despise wisdom and discipline. (Proverbs 1:7)

I have come that they may have life, and have it to the full. (John 10:10)

Do not be foolish but understand what the Lord's will is. (Ephesians 5:17)

Everything should be done in a fitting and orderly way. (1 Corinthians 14:40)

Submit to one another out of reverence for Christ. (Ephesians 5:21)

It is the Lord your God you must follow, and him you must revere. Keep his commands and obey him, serve him and hold fast to him. (Deuteronomy 13:4)

As for me and my household, we will serve the Lord. (Joshua 24:15)

Ascribe to the Lord the glory due his name. (1 Chronicles 16:29)

Therefore, I urge you brothers, in view of God's mercy, to offer your bodies as living sacrifices, holy and pleasing to God—this is your spiritual act of worship. (Romans 12:1)

Personal Reflection
As I reflect on this part of Paul's letter, this verse also comes to mind:

This day I call heaven and earth as witnesses against you that I have set before you life and death, blessings and curses. Now choose life, so that you and your children may live and that you may love the Lord your God, listen to his voice and hold fast to him. For the Lord is your life, and he will give you many years in the land he swore to your fathers, Abraham, Isaac and Jacob. (Deuteronomy 30:19-20)

This new life is our inheritance as believers. This Is God wanting to bless us and give our lives meaning, satisfaction, and fulfillment. We are here for such a short time. We're really just a blip on those screens we are so attached to today. We only have one life to live, so the choices we make every day count. All Jesus came to offer us is ours for the taking. He calls us to Himself and speaks to us as though we were the only one on earth. This is our inheritance that began with Abraham to make our life meaningful and productive (Genesis 12:1-3). This is the inheritance we are privileged to pass down to our children and our children's children until Jesus returns.

Personal Thoughts and Study Guide

1.   How would you describe order or lack of order in your life?

2.   What area of your life needs more order? What are you willing to change to bring it about?

3.   What gives you the most satisfaction and sense of purpose in your life and what motivates you to pursue it?

4. Which of Paul's strategies for a meaningful life can you incorporate so God's purpose for you is fulfilled?

5. What are you doing apart from God? How is that working out?

6. How would you describe your family relationships?

7. What can you take from Paul's teaching here to help them be better? Whom can you reach out to in your family?

8. How serious are you about praying for your family, your job, your interests, your conversations? Write out a prayer for each here or in the note section at the end of the book.

9. A meaningful life is ours to inherit. What will you take from this lesson to have more meaning in yours?

Make It your Own

Which Bible verse included will you memorize and recite each morning so each day has meaning for you and brings glory to God?

Hymn:

Take My Life and Let It Be
by Frances Havergal

Take my life, and let it be
Consecrated, Lord, to thee.
Take my moments and my days;
Let them flow in ceaseless praise.
Take my hands, and let them move
At the impulse of thy love.
Take my feet, and let them be
Swift and beautiful for thee.

Chapter 10

A Good Ending and
a Happy Homecoming

*O*ur life doesn't always end the way we thought it would or wanted it to. Paul certainly didn't want to be held prisoner in Rome in this last stage of his life. After all, he hadn't stopped preaching the gospel and helping people come to Christ since he was converted on the Road to Damascus. At that point, he had to reevaluate everything he had been programmed to know as a devout Jew. His personal encounter with Jesus changed his life forever. Every waking moment since had been devoted to spreading the good news of salvation to the known world. Now he is confined in prison. Now he is an old man. Time is slipping away. He could have easily chosen to have a royal pity party for himself. He could have easily chosen to spend his time bemoaning the fact he could be doing something far more significant than sitting in chains—like going on another missionary journey, or preaching in more synagogues, or seeing thousands more people come to Christ, or starting more churches. But at this point in his life that was not to be. God had so much more in mind. God had you and me in mind. God had every person born between then and now in mind. Little did Paul know the four letters he wrote during this time (including this one we are studying) would not only survive two thousand years but bless, challenge, comfort, and guide untold millions of people so that they, too, can claim the inheritance Jesus died to give them.

Thankfully, Paul did not give into pity or despair but followed God's leading and wrote this letter to the church in Colossae. As he closes this letter, he has no way of knowing how much time he has left. But his thoughts and concerns tell us he thinks it is coming to an end, and he doesn't want to waste a minute of it. He wants to finish strong. He wants to have a good ending to his earthly life even in the midst of very hard circumstances.

Here is our inheritance: Believers want to finish strong because they love Jesus and know a happy homecoming awaits them.

Paul wants this church to know even though he will never be able to visit them like he had hoped, God's kingdom had come to earth and nothing would stop it going forward. So his final words in this letter are words of encouragement, instruction, and farewell. He doesn't want to leave without saying good-bye to his friends and acknowledging their role in his life and ministry. Most of all, Paul wants them to remember the inheritance that is now theirs to enjoy.

The Bible says Paul said:

> Tychicus will tell you all the news about me. He is a dear brother, a faithful minister and fellow servant in the Lord. I am sending him to you for the express purpose that you may know about our circumstances and that he may encourage your hearts. He is coming with Onesimus, our faithful and dear brother, who is one of you. They will tell you everything that is happening here. (Colossians 4:7-9)

Knowing Our Inheritance

God's work is never done alone. He always surrounds His servants with like-minded people to accomplish His work. The ripple effect of one believer's life is far reaching and has eternal value for everyone involved. Without texting or email, we can only imagine the challenges of passing Paul's letter from this prison in Rome to the church in Colossae in Asia Minor, approximately 1,300 miles away. But Paul could count on his friends and fellow followers of Jesus, Tychicus and Onesimus, to deliver his letter. Paul knew these men well. He calls Tychicus a minister and both of them dear brothers, faithful, and fellow servants in the Lord. Paul knew nothing would prevent them from making this special delivery. He knew God wanted to encourage this church in Colossae. Therefore, Paul knew God would make it happen.

The Bible says Paul continues to say:

> My fellow prisoner Aristarchus sends you his greetings, as does Mark, the cousin of Barnabas. (You have received instructions about him; if he comes to you, welcome him.) Jesus, who is called Justus, also sends greetings. These are the only Jews among my fellow workers for the kingdom of God, and they have proved a comfort to me. Epaphras, who is one of you and a servant of Christ Jesus, sends greetings. He is always wrestling in prayer for you, that you may stand firm in all the will of God, mature and fully assured. I vouch for him that he is working hard for you and for those at Laodicea and Hierapolis. Our dear friend Luke, the doctor, and Demas send greetings. Give my greetings to the brothers at Laodicea, and to Nympha and the church in her house. (Colossians 4:10-15)

Receiving Our Inheritance

God always equips His servants for the work He calls them to do. He uses their different gifts and talents for His purpose and glory. Together, believers make a formidable team. Each one of these people Paul names is unique in their own right and a valuable team player in God's overarching plan to spread the good news of salvation in Jesus Christ to the then known world and beyond. Paul was known as the Apostle to the Gentiles or non-Jews. This group of people who worked with him so closely represented both Jews and Gentiles and would carry on after he was gone. We can learn from each of them.

Aristarchus was a Jew. He stayed with Paul through thick and thin. He was a longtime companion and friend. He was passionate about Jesus and helping Paul in his ministry.

Mark was also a Jew. He had had a rough beginning with Paul when he wanted to turn back from one of their missionary journeys. But all that was "old news" at this point, and Paul wanted the other churches to welcome him. As it turns out, Mark was the writer of the second gospel, the Gospel of Mark, in the New Testament.

Barnabas was Mark's cousin and to this day is known as "the encourager" because of the supporting role he played in the early church. We should all be known as a Barnabas.

Justus was also a Jew. He was the quiet, behind the scenes, faithful friend and coworker in Paul's ministry. Every team needs one.

Epaphras founded this church in Colossae and probably the sister churches in Laodicea and Hierapolis as well. Paul singles him out as the pray-er in this group, a wonderful reputation to have.

Luke was a Gentile. He was also a doctor and very close to Paul in his ministry. Later, Luke wrote the Gospel of Luke and the Book of Acts in the New Testament. He was a devoted friend and confidante to Paul and remained with him until the very end. (From Acts)

Demas started out well in his faith and traveling with Paul in his ministry, but when the going got tough, he loved the world more than he loved the Lord (2 Timothy 4:10). A sad ending, missed opportunity, and powerful lesson for us.

And Nympha held church in her own home. What courage!

These people all had the choice, just as we do, whether or not they wanted to finish strong with Jesus. They could have been content to stay comfortable in their own lives and circumstances. They could have been content just knowing they had eternal salvation in Jesus Christ. They could have rested in that knowledge and not done another thing to promote His kingdom. They could have let their fears for their own survival dictate their faith and their actions. And yet, with the exception of Demas, these people were like Paul. They were totally committed to Jesus. They had embraced their inheritance. They were proud of it and they were going to use it all up! Paul now gives them his final instructions.

The Bible says Paul said:

> After this letter has been read to you, see that it is also read in the church of the Laodiceans and that you in turn read the letter from Laodicea. Tell Archippus: "See to it that you complete the work you have received from the Lord." I, Paul, write this greeting in my own hand. Remember my chains. Grace be with you. (Colossians 4:16-18)

Living Our Inheritance

It is obvious Paul is not thinking of his own comfort, safety, or earthly future. He is now focused on how to get this letter to the church in Laodicea. Every ounce of his strength was going into making that happen. The church in Colossae had been invaded by false teachers who were compromising the purity of the gospel, and Paul undoubtedly wanted to thwart any efforts on their part to do the same in Laodicea. His instructions were firm. His example of conviction and commitment to his work for Jesus Christ is clearly communicated to brothers and sisters in the faith and coworkers in the ministry. Archippus was also a pastor and apparently needed Paul's encouragement to continue. Paul makes it clear that since the work Archippus was doing was the Lord's work in the first place, he needed to complete it. He needed to finish strong. We all do. We can all finish strong. We can complete the work God calls us to do as we claim the inheritance Jesus left us and spend it freely in our lives.

This was Paul's life commitment. This was what consumed him. He was actually released from prison this time, only to be taken prisoner again a few years later after refusing to back down from this commitment to share Christ. Even though he was never able to embark on a fourth missionary journey, Paul continued to share the inheritance we have in Jesus with everyone he met. He died committed to that task. His final letter was to Timothy who he called "his dear son" (2 Timothy 1:2). This time, Paul knew his time had come.

The Bible says Paul said:

> For I am already being poured out like a drink offering, and the time has come for my departure. I have fought the good fight, I have finished the race, I have kept the faith. Now there is in store for me the crown of righteousness, which the Lord, the righteous Judge, will award to me on that day—and not only to me, but also to all who have longed for his appearing. (2 Timothy 4:6-8)

That, my friends, is our inheritance. That is why we can get up every morning and bask in it. Only, and only in Jesus Christ, do we have: *The Gift of Salvation, Access to the Throne, Eternal Security, Fuel in our Tank, Strength for the Journey, Forgiveness, Freedom to Live, Peace in the Present, A Meaningful Life, A Good Ending and a Happy Homecoming.* Does it get any better than that?

Personal Reflection

A prayer I often pray is: "Lord, use me up before you take me home" because I don't want my faith to fizzle out toward the end of my life. I want it to grow and get stronger. No matter my condition or circumstances, I want to be a witness for Jesus until I see Him face to face. I am looking forward to my Happy Homecoming. How about you?

Bible verses to consider on our "departure":

> ... Death is the destiny of every man; the living should take this to heart. (Ecclesiastes 7:2)

> ... He will swallow up death forever. The Sovereign Lord will wipe away the tears from all faces ... (Isaiah 25:8)

> I tell you the truth, whoever hears my word and believes him who sent me has eternal life and will not be condemned; he has crossed over from death to life. (John 5:24)

> Where, O death, is your victory? Where, O death, is your sting? (1 Corinthians 15:55)

Even though I walk through the valley of the shadow of death, I will fear no evil, for you are with me; your rod and your staff, they comfort me. (Psalm 23:4)

For to me, to live is Christ and to die is gain. (Philippians 1:21)

He who believes in me will live even though he dies; and whoever lives and believes in me will never die. (John 11:25-26)

Precious in the sight of the Lord is the death of His saints. (Psalm 116:15)

And who doesn't want to hear these words:

Well done, good and faithful servant! (Matthew 25:21)

Personal Thoughts and Study Guide

1. Describe your life of faith from when you first received it until now.

2. What has helped you grow in your faith? What has hindered its growth?

3. How would your friends describe your faith? How would your family describe your faith?

4. Draw a graph to help you visualize the role your faith has played in your life.

5. What was going on in your life when it was at its peak? What was going on when it was at its lowest?

6. What are your spiritual goals so you will finish strong? How does Paul, and the friends he includes in this letter, inspire you to do so?

7. After studying Paul's letter to the Colossians, which of his warnings against false teaching will you take to heart to best protect yourself, your family, and your church from false teaching? Write them down so you can refer to them when you are concerned about what you are being taught.

8. How can you avoid the often attractive but false teachers who entice believers to their way of thinking?

Make It Your Own

Which Bible verse on our "departure" will you memorize for your comfort when you're facing your own death or to share with someone when they are facing theirs? Write it down to help you remember it.

The Bible is our inheritance. The gospel is our plumb line for living and for dying. Whom will you share this inheritance with so they, too, can have their share? God made sure there was enough for all who want to come to the cross to claim it.

Hymn:

To God be the Glory
by Frances J. Crosby

To God be the glory, great things He hath done,
So loved He the world that He gave us His Son,
Who yielded His life an atonement for sin,
And opened the life gate that all may go in.

Dear Reader,

Life in the twenty-first century is fast moving, competitive, stressful, and downright exhausting. It seems like we have lost our way. We are so tied to our screens there is little time in a twenty-four hour period to sit down and have a meaningful conversation with someone. Everything has to be shortened to accommodate our new "normal." Friends and even family members communicate by text so they can be doing two or three other things at the same time. Families seldom have dinner together because everyone is just too busy! The pressures of balancing home, work, school, family time, personal time, church time, community expectations, exercise, and a good night's sleep are becoming increasingly difficult, if not impossible.

This pressure we all feel begs these questions: Where are we going? What are we trying to accomplish? What can we do to slow down and relieve some of the pressure? What can we do to enjoy life more and be stressed out less? What can we do to make sure we are totally in sync with Jesus when He returns?

This book was written to that end. It was written to help us carve out a few minutes here and there to focus on the inheritance Jesus bequeathed to us. There is nothing in this world that compares to what we have in Him. Paul outlined it well in his letter to the church in Colossae two thousand years ago. It is up to us to know it, receive it, live it, and pass it on. That is my prayer for you, dear reader. Enjoy your inheritance while we wait for Jesus to return.

Candace Brown Doud
April 2018

Praise be to the God and Father of our Lord Jesus Christ! In his great mercy he has given us new birth into a living hope through the resurrection of Jesus Christ from the dead, and into an inheritance that can never perish, spoil or fade—kept in heaven for you ... 1 Peter 1:3-5

Acknowledgements

*S*tudying the Bible brings us face-to-face with our need for Jesus Christ and God's plan for our life. I am eternally grateful to Bible Study Fellowship, a worldwide teaching ministry, for their commitment to teaching the Bible with this goal in mind. As a class member, then in leadership, and later as a Teaching Leader, the knowledge and training I received through this organization was, and continues to be, life changing.

To Jim, my husband of fifty-five years, and my entire family, for your continued love, prayers, support, and encouragement. Thank you!

To my many friends and fellow believers who are always quick to pray and encourage. Thank you!

To my editors, Linda Wagner and Debbie Austin, for your professional expertise, but also for the friendships we have forged and your own journeys of faith you have shared. Thank you!

To Tom Brewer, for lending your keen mind, knowledge of God's Word, and strong faith to this study. Thank you!

And most of all, to Jesus, my Lord and my God, thank You for allowing me this privilege. It is for Your honor and glory—until You return!

CPSIA information can be obtained
at www.ICGtesting.com
Printed in the USA
FSHW01n0006200618
49457FS

9 781545 635933